9 Winning Habits of Successful Software Sales Professionals

How to strategically close sales deals in a fierce competitive market

Dr. Raghu Korrapati, Ph.D., D.Sc., D.Litt.

DIAMOND BOOKS

www.diamondbook.in

Publisher : **Diamond Pocket Books (P) Ltd.**
X-30, Okhla Industrial Area, Phase-II
New Delhi-110020

Phone : 011-40712200
E-mail : sales@dpb.in
Website : www.diamondbook.in
Editorials : Saif Nadeem

9 Winning Habits of Successful Software Sales Professionals

By – Dr. Raghu Korrapati

Contact the Author:
Website: http://www.raghukorrapati.com
E-mail: raghu.korrapati@gmail.com
Phone: +1- (803) 422 6397 EDT **Fax:** +1-(866) 292 1949

a

Dedicated to

Arvindram, Ganeshram, & Arya

Parents and Grand Parents

Preface

It is often said that salespeople would rather sell than spend a day learning how to do it. They think time is money and every hour spent in training is money lost and time wasted. But what they fail to understand is that learning how to do sales effectively is actually a catalyst for great sales results for the organization and excellent sales performance for the individual. It is worth noting that while sales is one of the easiest careers to get into, but it is not as easy to sustain and spend a life in. So to put it in simpler words,

"Everyone can be a sales person, but not everyone can be a successful sales person"

To be a successful salesperson it is important to have a deep understanding of the industry you cater to. While the general skill set remains the same, it is the deeper and niche understanding that has the power to differentiate the best from the rest.

Top performing companies highly rely on software to stay ahead of competition, especially the nimble and cost-effective version, Software as a Service (SaaS). As the companies race to leverage software, the demand is soaring. To meet this demand, Software companies are building best in class sales teams, to generate more revenue, profits and value for investors, quickly.

Success in sales depends on your ability to find or generate leads, build relationships and close sales. It requires willingness to compete with other sales professionals and a lot of hustle. As companies rely on sales professionals for their survival and leadership in the industry, effective sales professionals experience rapid upward mobility in their careers as well as in compensation.

In the market, there are numerous books and articles on various sales techniques available. In this book, I am discussing the 'Nine habits of highly effective software sales professionals'. The title gives you a broad idea of what this book is all about, but more than nine habits, it is packed with 30 years of my personal and professional experience in the software industry and managing clients. I provided more emphasis on how successful sales professionals, sales leaders and their companies organize themselves with short-term and long-term planning and adopt disciplined execution on those plans.

I have had the privilege of managing a broad range of clients ranging from world class IT companies to some of the largest insurance companies in the world. My experience in software sales expands across cultures, geography and language – from India and Asia Pacific to the Americas and Europe. I have worked with many whom I consider some of the best sales professionals during these years. They have brought in millions of dollars by selling software products and services across a range of clients worldwide by solving their business problems through those offerings. It is from that experience I have extracted nine habits that every sales professional must display to make the journey from a sales person to a 'successful sales professional'.

Finally, I believe that in one-word sales is "Managing Expectations of All Stake Holders" – his or her customers, organization, family and team, balancing their requirements effectively and efficiently. For example, customer demands price reduction at better quality, organization needs to maximize revenue and profits, family demands more time, team needs more benefits etc., so you have to manage all these expectations effectively and efficiently.

I sincerely believe that this book is a 'must-have' for every student who is studying software and IT, every college/institute that imparts these courses, every fresher sales person in the software industry, every experienced sales professional who wants to lead a team in the future, every software and services sales manager who wants to make his/her team perform more effectively and to deliver better results. I have also shared my thoughts on how sales organizations can enable successful sales operations through systems and processes.

I hope this book will help usher in more success in your career.

Happy Selling!

Contents

Introduction

Sales is one of the most competitive and potentially the most lucrative professions today. The work is rather challenging. Hours are long. Management of ever-growing expectations and desires of clients and sales managers can be frustrating and the fierce need to perform and drive revenue is relentless. Being a sales professional isn't easy and not everyone can work in sales. If there is one crucial aspect that characterizes exceptionally successful sales professional, it is their emphasis on persistently raising their execution by recognizing and cascading best practices in all parts of their business, with a specific end goal to successfully overcome any hindrances in all engagements, time and again.

Software sales representatives must demonstrate some specific key skills. With more than thirty years of experience in corporate management as well as academic understanding of the various evolving concepts in software sales, I've written this book with an aim to provide some fundamental and highly effective habits of sales professionals. Throughout this book, I've shared habits of very successful sales professionals and sales operations leaders, and talked about how you can utilize these habits to help improve your own particular execution.

In the following section, I will discuss some of the most commonly discussed traits about sales person, which will act as the foundation to the traits of a successful software sales professional:

1. 'How can I help?' v-s. 'What can I sell?'

You can distinguish from the average sales people at an early point in the cycle by a simple yet very effective shift in the approach. As the pressure to sell and close a deal is very strong and continues to increase ever, they often look at the prospects or clients as a means to achieve their end – meeting or exceeding sales quota. However, exceptionally good sales professionals like the one you want to become, approach clients by asking themselves - "How can I help this client?". Clients are often very quick to notice this difference in style and tend to open up more thus paving the foundation for a long and mutually successful business relationship.

2. Ask more questions and listen more carefully & Understand your prospect thoroughly

You can avoid one of the most common mistakes that sales professionals make with clients – claiming to know more about client's problems and its solutions than they truly do. Average sales people focus on the wrong kind of question i.e. "What would I be able to sell?" They use such question in order to set up the offer that they had pre-decided in their mind even before they called on the client. This narrow and shallow approach quite often leads to poor or suboptimal sales, and in some cases loss of a sale completely. You can change this narrative by coming prepared to ask comprehensive set of questions by following best practices in information gathering techniques and listen to your client more carefully. Analyze the responses to get a better understanding and perspective of client's true needs and offer software and any related services that would bring real value and deliver the desired business outcomes for them.

3. Sell value price

Due to the constant pressure to increase revenue, most sales people are comfortable with the compulsion to provide concession or give ground on different terms and conditions, keeping in mind the end goal is to win the business. This is especially evident when the customers demand incentives for closing the deal before the month end or year end. The end of month setting is quick; most sales people will take the money and run, particularly in a down economy, regardless of whether it implies surrendering profit margins to do it. You can become an exceedingly productive sales professional when you realize that your company depends on healthy profit margins and brand reputation to thrive in the marketplace, and take the additional time to explain the value to the customer in a way they can appreciate and agree. Most customers are willing to pay higher premium for software and services that offer such value to their business.

3. Adapt and get creative

As a highly successful sales professional, you should recognize that customers simply don't buy products, they buy solutions. This is where average sales people fail to perform because they are narrowly focused on selling products. Indeed, even when selling most commoditized products, expert sales professionals believe that when you can make choices that are lined up with the client's needs, you can make your product a piece of a bigger picture solution. It is more likely that the customer will discover such proposition all the more engaging and worth pursuing. Never ignore to investigate thoughts and alternatives that are unique and outside the normal realm.

4. Build connections over the entire client organization

In any sales process, the attention is by and large on recognizing the decision maker(s) and doing whatever you can to get before them with your offer. Beyond any doubt it is difficult to finalize negotiations without the help of the chief. Identifying the key decision maker in a negotiation can also be tricky. In his book "Never Split The Difference", author Chris Voss emphasizes the fact that key decision makers in a negotiation are shrewd in hiding their influence. He states that such people try to make themselves seem powerless in a negotiation and use words like "they", "them". The more such people try to deflect attention away from themselves, the more likely it is that they have got a good amount of decision power. Be that as it may, in many organizations, the decision maker is associated with and supported by a bigger system such as purchase gate keepers, enterprise wide program management office and so on. Exceptionally effective sales professionals keep in mind the need to create connections and trust with the bigger system so as to pick up knowledge of the exact requirement to develop their offer when they finally get before the decision maker.

6. Set Goals

Average sales professionals time and again let their pipelines set their motivation, doing as well as can be expected to catch up on whatever leads fall into their laps and striving to close whatever business they can in any way it comes to them. In contrast, profoundly successful sales experts are result driven. They understand what they require to finish through a progression of quantifiable objectives, and they design their client systems and exercises to concentrate on accomplishing those results. Successful Venture Capitalist - John Doerr - promoted the idea of Objectives and Key Results (OKRs) in his book - "Measure What Matters". OKRs are a great way not only to align the "What" with "How" and keep the sales goals aligned with overall company goals but also to stay focused on the steps to achieve those set goals. As a successful sales professional you can certainly utilize pipeline as a guide and an asset, but you must additionally refine and organize that pipeline with a specific end goal i.e. to accomplish the results you are going for. For very effective sales professionals, time and domain administration isn't a popular expression utilized as a part of offers gatherings. It is an instrument that characterizes what accounts they will seek after, and when and how they will seek after them. In the event that anytime they establish that their exercises are not meeting their objectives, they rapidly update, reload, and start from the very beginning once more. They never dawdle on exercises that don't create prompt, quantifiable outcomes.

7. Measure outcomes regularly and genuinely

Some regular sales personnel can't deal with reality. They are awkward with channel audits and assessment sessions unless they have had a decent month and the assessment is positive. At the point when the numbers are off, they feel disappointed and their nervousness level goes up. Whereas exceptionally productive sales experts comprehend that the key to progress is in the numbers – great or awful. Are the numbers up? Great, discover why and continue utilizing that for more achievement. Are the numbers down? Try not to freeze, discover why and fix it. Exceedingly successful sales professionals measure everything, not only the estimation of the deals flow toward the end of the month. Measuring and assessing each sale with each client will help reveal reality and indicate the path toward more achievement.

8. Develop responsibility

Sales professionals are energized (and somewhat diminished) at whatever point they make it happen. Exceedingly effective sales experts are normally happy, however they comprehend something that a ton of less experienced sales persons don't understand: letting the big dog eat is basically one sway to significantly more prominent achievements so that they will just remain focused on winning the client's business.

Exceedingly good sales experts burn through roughly 10% of their assets teaching the universe. They invest 30% of their energy developing associations for forthcoming clients. Yet, they spend an incredible 60% of their time and imaginative vitality proceeding to develop trust and explore openings with existing clients. It costs five times the amount of time and effort to offer another client as it does to make a similar deal to a current client. Commonly, the tenth buy from a current client is 80% bigger than the primary buy. As a skilled sales expert, you will remain in consistent contact with your current clients to ensure that the software or services they purchased is functioning admirably, and to rapidly address any inquiries or issues that emerge. Treat clients more like companions than as mere sources of income. By one means or another, it generally pays off.

9. Keep up an inspirational state of mind

We have effectively called attention to the fact that offering can be an intense business. At the point when the economy is down or market forces are not allowing sales to close, sales persons begin hearing a great deal of "No's," which can destroy their confidence on occasions. It isn't unnatural for the average sales professionals to question their aspirations or their capacities on occasions this way. Highly efficient sales representatives don't let temporary misfortunes to characterize them. Rather, their trust in themselves, their offering allow them to stay inspired. Their interesting mix of certainty, hopefulness, energy, notwithstanding here and now challenges, drives them to search for circumstances when others are rationalizing. The ability to stay focused during the times of crisis is a great skill to possess and nurture.

10. Perform everything with respectability & Ethically

There is a marginally awkward dynamic that appears to keep running out of sight of numerous connections amongst client and sales professionals. Most clients don't like being "sold to," so they can be somewhat shut and even suspicious in a business relationship. To break through this protection, sales personnel now and then want to fall back on unpretentious types of control to help let the big dog eat. Average sales person may win a couple of deals along these lines, yet he/she isn't probably going to win some long term clients. Profoundly effective sales professionals understand that it takes transparency, trustworthiness, and an unmistakable absence of self-intrigue to make the level of trust with a client important to build a strong relationship and nurture it. This incorporates not just conveying great features or benefits of the offerings on time and as guaranteed, but also requires raising up to the occasion and working with the client to settle issues rapidly and bring real business value.

11. Continue to learn and build up your abilities and never stop

The business field is brimming with individuals who view themselves as specialists. They have numerous times of involvement and they have amassed an awesome measure of product learning. Regardless of that, a large number of them fail to meet expectations, and as a rule this issue is caused by the way that a business professional trusts himself/herself to be such a specialist. This not only prompts carelessness or complacency, but also prompts the genuine probability that they will be left behind by other individuals who continually hone their abilities and use new advances to make points of interest where others discover snags. We call these other individuals, "profoundly efficient sales professional". This will lead an individual to 'consultative sales professional' to a 'commodity sales professional'.

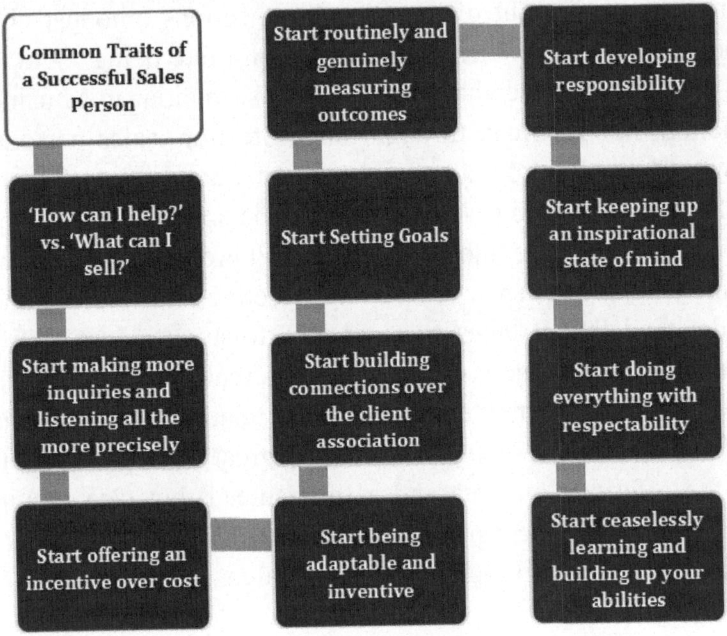

Fig: 1 – Most common traits that a successful sales person must imbibe

Software Sales

Computers would be pointless without the software that keep running on them. Regardless of the type of software—operating systems or any other kind, the sales in software and services run into hundreds of billions of dollars. Furthermore, software and related services sales professionals are individuals who work beyond the sales on the Internet and the big local stores. Their job requires them to have a special skill set that would enable large software companies to sell their product or services to potential customers, especially to those looking for large scale software solution.

Software sales experts are accountable for making sale of particular kinds of software, which is often designed for a specific type of industry. The software intended for the administrative purposes in a dental specialist office would be a good example of industry-specific software. Furthermore, in all likelihood, the sales representative pitching the software to the dental practitioners of the world just sells software to dentists. The explanation behind this specialty is to ensure that the business experts know the software product in depth. These specially crafted software sales professionals are quite often viewed as expensive.

Software sales professionals earn big salaries, provided they make necessary sales! The shortcoming with these positions is that sales cycles are normally very long, making the time between commission checks similarly extended. Thus, the software sales is a profession which is demanding and requires an individual to have the confidence on their ability to deliver on sales goals.

In addition to selling software, successful sales professionals find ways to bundle it with related services that a business will require and can benefit from. Without an Information Technology (IT) expert or a group of specialists on staff that are knowledgeable and experienced in successfully utilizing the software it buys, businesses cannot reap the benefits. So they will require help exploring their way in the form of software services. Such services are widely called as IT Services. This then becomes an avenue for gaining extraordinary pay. Services come in many structures, from the basic services of implementing the software system to provide consulting services to an organization as they consider virtualizing their own data center to transform the business. Service extends incredibly, as do the pay capability of those offering them. Services are the adhesive holding IT sales world together. Those in IT service sales sometimes offer hardware solutions, combined with software packaged with established services. Most IT service sales experts work with a group of experts who are specialists in specific areas of the IT world, thus avoiding the costly burden of being a specialist in everything.

In the next few chapters, there will be a detailed discussion of nine habits that a software sales professionals must incorporate in their day to day life. These chapters are designed to give budding sales personnel as well as experienced professionals an overview of the traits they must inculcate to increase the sales of various software and services provided by their companies. Here you will learn the need for qualities for "show and tell" of software services to buyers around the world.

1. Doing the right thing

Customers demand sales professionals who are trustworthy and willing to hold themselves to account. They also expect them to add value to their business. Meanwhile salespeople are under increasing pressure from their managers to maximize sales, customers/prospects to reduce the price and from regulators to be compliant. To reconcile these competing demands, sales professionals daily have to make difficult judgments, based on complex and ethical dilemmas.

The most significant part of any job is the sense of integrity in the person. Like other professional jobs, sales professionals must understand the significance of ethics and follow a certain standard of conduct. According to the Association of Professional Sales, in order to do the right thing, one must demonstrate the following qualities:

1. Maintain the highest standards of integrity in all business relationships.
2. Provide customers with an excellent buying experience in which we "do the right thing and thereby get the right results".
3. Promote and protect good sales practices.
4. Always act in line with organization's code of conduct and within the law.

The sales code of ethics is a much talked about issue and

various governing bodies around the world have asserted that there needs to be a standardized code of ethics across all sales and marketing professional positions. One of the most notable set of ethical codes was established by Sales and Marketing Executives Inc. (SMEI), which pledged the following:

1. I hereby acknowledge my accountability to the organization for which I work and to society as a whole to improve sales knowledge and practice and to adhere to the highest professional standards in my work and personal relationships.
2. My concept of selling includes as its basic principle the sovereignty of all consumers in the marketplace and the necessity for mutual benefit to both buyer and seller in all transactions.
3. I shall personally maintain the highest standards of ethical and professional conduct in all my business relationships with customers, suppliers, colleagues, competitors, governmental agencies, and the public.
4. I pledge to protect, support, and promote the principles of consumer choice, competition, and innovation enterprise, consistent with relevant legislative public policy standards.
5. I shall not knowingly participate in actions, agreements, or marketing policies or practices, which may be detrimental to customers, competitors, or established community social or economic policies or standards.
6. I shall strive to ensure that products and services are distributed through such channels and by such methods as will tend to optimize the distributive process by offering maximum customer value and service at minimum cost while providing fair and equitable compensation for all parties.
7. I shall support efforts to increase productivity or reduce costs

of production or marketing through standardization or other methods, provided these methods do not stifle innovation or creativity.

8. I believe prices should reflect true value in use of the product or service to the customer, including the pricing of goods and services transferred among operating organizations worldwide.
9. I acknowledge that providing the best economic and social product value consistent with cost also includes: (a) recognizing the customer's right to expect safe products with clear instructions for their proper use and maintenance; (b) providing easily accessible channels for customer complaints; (c) investigating any customer dissatisfaction objectively and taking prompt and appropriate remedial action; (d) recognizing and supporting proven public policy objectives such as conserving energy and protecting the environment.
10 I pledge my efforts to assure that all marketing research, advertising, and presentations of products, services, or concepts are done clearly, truthfully, and in good taste so as not to mislead or offend customers. I further pledge to assure that all these activities are conducted in accordance with the highest standards of each profession and generally accepted principles of fair competition.
11. I pledge to cooperate fully in furthering the efforts of all institutions, media, professional associations, and other organizations to publicize this creed as widely as possible throughout the world.

Professionalism is one of the key topics in modern software sales ethics. There are numerous elements involved, including the expansion of proficient sales bodies for codes of conduct, which can be used to standardize and regulate members in the profession, more specifically sales professional in software companies. The significance of a code of ethics cannot be asserted enough; a sales professional is only as good as his/her word. As software sales professional, you will be furthermore expected to have the ability to distinguish 'right' from 'wrong'. 'Right' is evaluated in terms of ethical conduct of the sales professional. Every sales professional must understand the importance of the code of conduct and ethics in acquiring potential business and maintaining the relationship with those clients.

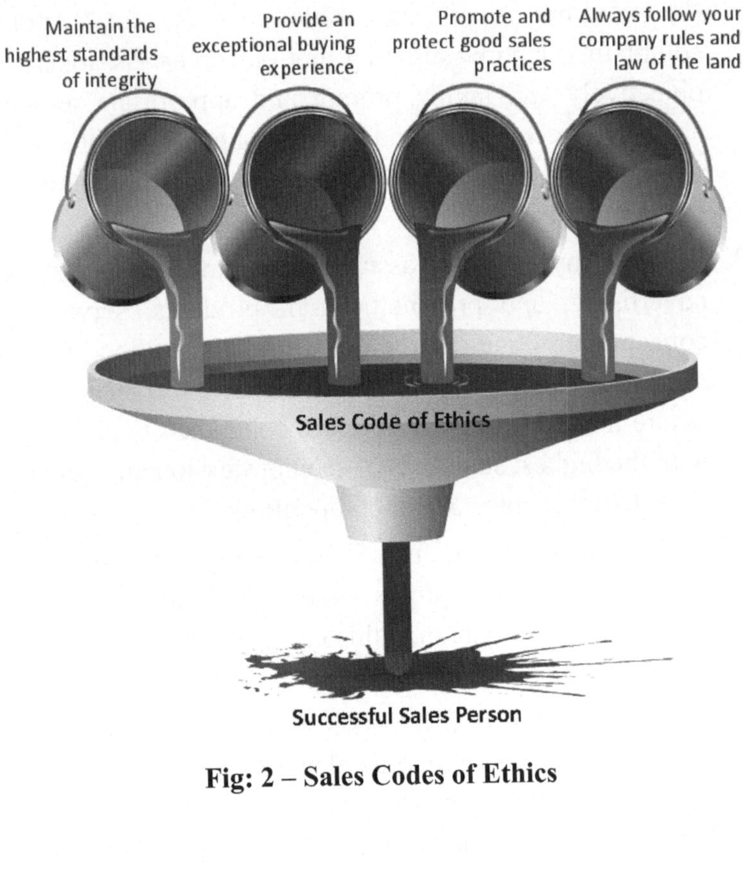

Fig: 2 – Sales Codes of Ethics

2. Living by 100- day plan

"Long-range planning works best in the short term"

- Doug Evelyn

As an IT sales professional, the first 100-day duration is an extremely crucial period in terms of functionality. Thus, the first 100 days must be used wisely. Most of the success you will have in the first few years in such a role will be determined by how effectively you use the first 100 days. Against the common misconception, the first three months are not merely for review and observation, rather it is for unrelenting hard work and activity that are result driven. There's an old adage that sales professionals *who fail to plan are probably unaware that they are planning to fail!*

In order to make a powerful 100 days design, you have to realize the focus area for these days. Identify this focus area from introspection and from the discussions with your colleagues. When you realize that, you make 30, 60, and 90 days quantifiable plans of how you will make progress in those focus areas to reach your sales objectives. It ends up simply continuing and regularly measuring your advances regarding the deal pipeline each day. When you are finished with the first 100 day design, repeat this action and make the following one for the next 100 days and so on.

Before you make your Plan, try the following:

Stay calm

The primary task is to stay levelheaded and calm. Leaping into the clamor will do more harm than help. It is best not to feel pressured into rushing things, which would eventually lead to making poor decisions. Have some quality time alone every day. Alone means with none other than yourself. Nobody else. Not the group, nor the family. Not even any other kind of media. Just yourself. You require time to think, time to organize, plan and prepare a timetable. Make the time, before anything else or even better, last thing in night. At whatever point it is effective for you; simply make sure it happens.

Analyze the situation

The second aspect of getting your initial 100-day design is to apply your diagnostic aptitudes as a powerful influence for the circumstance. Here you have to evaluate: What have you learned? What is great about your new operation and what is terrible? It won't be basically high contrast. There'll be shades of dark. Utilize the accompanying Six Ps to get an outline of where you stand.

- **Plans:** Comprehend top to bottom what the organization's designs are- strategies for success, promoting plans, software or services/its benefit, dispatch designs, long-term plans, short-term plans, and web based business designs or any others. You need to know where the objective posts are, and where your commitment will fit. Utilize this part to get a genuine reason on what is anticipated from you by your company. Plan and analyze how, as a sales personnel of your company, you can make a difference and achieve the sales target.
- **Participants:** You need time to think and organize. Time to plan and establish a definite timetable. Make a

timetable and make sure you stick by it. Team leaders and managers know that their products are of not much use without good sales person supporting them. Your first meeting with the managers is not about sales deals execution - or its absence, it is about your potential. You must disclose to them your plans, however most importantly, ensure you have tuned in to them. At that point get out in the field with them. You need to perceive how they offer and build their customer connections. You won't have the capacity to mentor them or offer suggestions if you haven't seen their qualities and shortcomings.

- **Pipeline:** Your initial days in the company presents a good opportunity to evaluate the potential business. Odds are it looks depressing. Numerous business administration substitutions happen on the grounds that the business execution is under standard. Approach your business agents for their present pipeline conjectures. And after that make extensive inquiries. The sooner they know you won't endure dream or theory, the sooner they'll quit serving it up to you. Get every individual to give you a point by point rundown on each of their main three key records. Search for how they approach this undertaking – it will give you criticism on how deliberately they are functioning with the organization's key source of income and benefits. Ask them what they perceive as blockers in the business. In the event that you can give them some 'convenient solutions', at that point you will straight away begin to strike as smart colleague.
- **Procedures:** Take a look at the methods and procedures you have acquired. They may be flawed and you may need them changed down the track, however for now you need to consider the following:

- ✓ What is the present sales forecasting regime?
- ✓ When are the projections due from your group?
- ✓ What are the disciplines related with quoting, bidding and tendering?
- ✓ What activity report is needed from the team?
- ✓ What key account plan is utilized?
- ✓ What sales plans do the group have and how are they utilized?
- ✓ What are the parameters of your budgetary authority?
- ✓ How does the sales incentive and reward structure function?

- ✓ **Products and Services:** You have to know whether your offering and contracts convey what they guarantee. Is there input from clients or customers? Make sure you comprehend the great focuses and the poor spots.
- ✓ **Playing field:** What do you think about your offerings in the market? How do your software and services stand out in the market and benefit clients? How's your estimation holding up? Who are the objective clients and why? Knowing the playing field likewise implies keeping current with industry trends and aligning your sales positioning accordingly.

You need to create a monthly, quarterly or yearly sales plan. It is a must. Begin with existing customers and put forth the flowing inquiries:

- What extent of the business income target was accomplished a year ago from existing customers?
- What potential is there from existing customers during the current year?
- How will I keep in contact with these current customers

to offer some benefit and purpose behind them to do a similar sum or extra measures of business with me this year?

- What sum do I have to discover from new customers?
- How will I distinguish these new customers?
- What promoting and sales exercises have I or others used to secure business with existing customers?
- What sales exercises and methodologies will I utilize to set up arrangements or reach in different courses with the potential customers, to find and illuminate where there may be potential for me to make an incentive for them?

When you have addressed these inquiries, you are ready to advance and have the capacity to finish your 100-day design. Once you've distinguished the exercises that you will embrace, it's then a procedure of getting more specific about what you will do on a month-to-month, fortnightly, weekly basis for the following 100 days.

A major aspect of the 100-day planning process is to track your progress towards the end of every week. This might be a self-survey of how you went about the accomplishments you planned for, or it could be talking about your progress with a partner or your manager.

You can achieve 100-day plan by staying focused on your sales targets. In the event your 100-day actions will give you the greatest probability of accomplishing or beating your objective, concentrate the majority of your energy on planning the next 100 days.

Here's a tip for succeeding in 100-day plan execution. Try not to smack yourself for what you did, or didn't do, 100 days prior. It's your day's task that is imperative. When you acknowledge this course, it's considerably less demanding to drive forward despite dips. To make a solid, steady, consistent, 100-day design dependably be considering and working 100 days out.

Ask the following questions to know your key focus areas for making 100-day plans:

- Do you hold staff meetings at the same time and place every week?
- Do you tell the team how the group is doing and how the team fits into the bigger picture of the company?
- Do you conduct sales meetings once a month or at least once a quarter?
- Do you work with your team in a sales target setting and conduct reviews?
- Do you ensure that your team understands how everyone's work relates to the business' sales mission?
- Do you provide your employees ways to improve their sales effectiveness or performance?
- Do you have a scheduled one-on-one meeting at least once every two weeks with your team to discuss issues and concerns?
- Do you define clear goals and link them to organizational goals?
- Do you encourage team members to look for the most innovative way to deal with a potential customer request?
- Do you find out success stories within the company that emphasize teamwork and share them?

Since the first 100 days is the most critical predictor of your success at any job, you will need to learn the software and its related services inside and out, be able to communicate it to prospects, and meanwhile, find your own leads to talk to.

The following section discusses various characteristic checklists that can be helpful in the 100-day plan.

DAY 1: Learning about the company and software products

Regardless of if this is your first or your tenth sales job, the first day is certainly an exciting one. It includes adapting new things about the organization's software products and services, culture, procedures, and group. Take the following couple of days endeavoring to retain and learn as much as you can from your managers and partners. Be proactive and demonstrate that you're willing to learn. Above all, take notes.

Checklist

- ✓ **Do you like this organization?** In the event that you don't, continue looking. Ensure you like what the organization is, the product, the service and what it stands for.
- ✓ **Spend time with your supervisor**: Learn about the core issues, assets that are accessible, your needs and objectives, and how you will be assessed. This will be the best time to clear any ambiguities and document them.
- ✓ **Customer records**: Ask your sales director whether you can get a rundown of about 30 or so current clients to gain a perspective of how things are running with every client and what they like and don't care for about the software and company. Offer any uplifting news with the business group promptly. Make a list of 30 or so former clients and ask them what the organization could have done to keep their business.

- ✓ **Be an example from day** 1: Meet with as many colleagues as you can and ensure that they consider you to be a resource for the business and for themselves.
- ✓ **Become a specialist**: It's important that you teach yourself on the software products and services that you will offer. Also understand your industry and normal issues your software solves and its differentiators in the market.

Day 6 – Learning more about your clients

After you've set yourself up and are up to speed with how things function at your organization, set aside opportunity to find out about the client that you will work with. Regardless of whether this is an industry that you've worked in and consummated sales to some clients recently, it is essential to comprehend the complexities and details relating to the interest of your clients and how you serve them.

Checklist

- ✓ Consult and coordinate with your clients. They can give awesome insights about your market that will enable you to quickly learn about what they like and what's resonating well with target clients.
- ✓ Build a profile of your clients, their business, their issues, and how they benefit from your software products and services.
- ✓ Write down a FABs (Feature, Advantage, Benefit) review of all the features of software and services that you can offer.

Day 11 – Get your hands dirty with sales meetings and conferences

Since you've overcome the initial 10 days, build on this

momentum to begin learning about how software sales functions at your organization. There are many steps to finishing a software sales deal: working with the CRM (Customer Relationship Management) software, contacting the lead, influencing the sales deals at calls/meetings, finalizing the negotiations, and sending the contracts, which will all be your responsibility. Spend the following week shadowing sales calls and following up for sales meetings. Give careful consideration to how they decide a warm lead, the sorts of inquiries that clients have, how the sales people present deals, and how they get ready for potential clients' meetings.

When you feel sufficiently certain, begin connecting with a few prospects to initiate involvement. You'll rapidly find your style and figure out how to think and react quickly while handling the sales calls. It's additionally vital to not accept that the current process is the best suited, so shadow more than two colleagues, and if possible shadow your manager. Accommodate what's unique and see where you might be able to set up your own style.

Checklist

- ✓ Shadow 5 software sales calls.
- ✓ Attend 3 software sales meetings.
- ✓ Make 25 cold calls.
- ✓ Recognize 10 trigger occasions for your clients.
- ✓ At the end of the week, build up a 100-day plan with your supervisor.

Concede to the expectations of the company and prioritize accordingly.

Day 16 – Building your pipeline

Software sales deals are a game of numbers. The more qualified prospects you get to the highest point of the business channel, the more sales deals you'll have the capacity to close at the center of bottom of the channel. Just like in any other industry, for software sales you will need to locate that specific channel which is more successful for prospecting than others. Invest significant time and energy in getting set up and looking into which channels will work best for you.

For starters, take a look at your present network. Having switched over from one company to another is a good opportunity to reconnect with your circle and to keep up your relationship intact. Connect with contacts with whom you have stayed in touch and those who would be interested or invested to find out about your new endeavors. Reveal to them your new role and welcome any referrals. Ensure they know you are looking forward to return the favor if and when the need arises. This is a great way to work on confidence, practice and eliminate any stress from the situation.

Checklist

- ✓ Identify 10 warm leads in your CRM that the organization has in their records and meet them.
- ✓ Attend 2 software related events and network in them.
- ✓ Reconnect with 10 contacts in your system to inform them regarding your new profile.

Day 21 – Getting started with inquiry and online networking

Social media is a good place to start and expand your network range. Organizations and individuals tend to trust and work with people who they know and trust. Social media is a great way to let people get acquainted with not only you but also the company you work for. Online networking is an incredible route for you to unpretentiously get associated, find out about them, and get yourself noted. Explore Twitter, LinkedIn, and whatever other social media sources that could be compelling. While you're busy, set up some Google Alerts with the keywords that you conceptualized from Day 11. This will help you to stay in touch with the news, events and occasions in your industry.

Checklist

- ✓ Set up Twitter account and follow relevant people.
- ✓ Sign up and finish LinkedIn profile to 100%.
- ✓ Get Quora, Google+, and Facebook accounts.
- ✓ Find and subscribe to 5 important web journals or blogs.
- ✓ Set up 10 Google alerts for important key terms.

Advanced Checklist

- ✓ Create your own blog through free tool like WordPress and write blog post based on the identified need of potential clients and the software solution that your company can offer.
- ✓ Using Twitter and other social media follow contacts belonging to specific companies. Interact with them and show interest in their work and segment them into the list.

Day 31 – Building a habit of time management

The primary thing you can control in your day is what number of messages, calls and meetings you can get. The response to meeting targets is two things: MORE and BETTER.

Increase the volume of your financial gains and improve your presentations and be more efficient. Investing energy in assignments, for example, instantly answering to insignificant messages, conversing with inadequate leads, or getting stood up as a result of unverified gatherings will deplete your business efficiency by half. Begin building solid time administration propensities.

Here is some insight in time management and how you can apply it to your sales week.

- Attempt to plan your meeting before anything else, just earlier or after lunch, or last thing in the day.
- Complete your target for the day before moving to do anything else. After you have made your last call, email or meeting, you have one more thing to do: make a note of what you did that day.

It's important that you measure your execution in the initial 100 days. In the event that you are behind on sales deal, meeting amounts or route ahead, you know the volume of monetary standards it took to get you there. You'll comprehend what you have to do to improve the situation the following quarter. Try not to GUESS and DON'T BE LAZY. You can control your prosperity in the event that you simply measure and make strides. You can't measure if you don't keep a record of it. So be diligent and dedicated.

If you've completed the day's quota, nothing is preventing you from achieving more prospects, however this time ought to really be saved for examining, perusing, taking a shot at making inbound movement through online networking and booking your plan for the next day.

Checklist

- ✓ Create a timetable for the following week from now with blocked times for different sales activities. Be disciplined to not get occupied while working in those time blocks.

- ✓ Track, measure and think about sales for every quota for a period of time —days, weeks and months.

Day 36 – Using online networking mediums for prospecting and sales deals

Online networking and prospecting exercises can rapidly get out of hand when you're on different channels and speaking with numerous individuals. A smart thought is to utilize tools that aggregate and manage all these exercises in a single place. Online networking dashboards, RSS readers, and notifications will enable you to remain over your activities notwithstanding when you're off making calls.

Checklist

- ✓ Setup RSS channel on Google Reader and read from 5 websites.
- ✓ Subscribe to LinkedIn answers for your important classes.
- ✓ Read posts discussing how to utilize online networking for prospecting
- ✓ Find 15 prospects on LinkedIn.
- ✓ Follow 5 organizations on LinkedIn.
- ✓ Follow 25 individuals on Twitter.
- ✓ Ask for 5 customer referrals.

Day 46 – Giving an incentive to get value

The online buzz on social media is all about value. As a software sales professional, you have an intensive comprehension of various issues affecting businesses and distinctive trends that are on the rise among various businesses. Share your insights with others and build a following.

Checklist

- ✓ Answer 15 inquiries on LinkedIn, Quora, Focus, or a gathering that is more important to software industry.
- ✓ Share your solutions to your informal community and request that they join the discussion or for their input.
- ✓ Engage in discussions with 10 unique individuals through Twitter. Retweet their substance, answer an inquiry, or add to a dialog.
- ✓ Using different channels, share content originating from your organization blog. Thus creating an online presence for your company and a buzz around the software solution available. This attracts potential businesses and creates awareness.

Day 61 – Establishing yourself as a pioneer in the space

An extraordinary method to construct a brand and engage with others online is to draw in with pioneers and leaders in the space. The key is to interact with the people who have a following in the area of software solutions or the IT services market. Invest time in similar sites and comment on their posts to establish a relationship. The same can be also done on Twitter, LinkedIn, and different portals where you can Retweet, Like, and Share their comments.

Checklist

- ✓ Identify and buy in to 5 pertinent sites (tail them on Twitter on the off chance that they are utilizing it).
- ✓ Read a couple of their current blogs and leave a comment on each blog that adds to that point.
- ✓ Send an individual email to each writer and connect on a subject that they have expounded on where you may have some learning to share.

- ✓ Follow 25 influencers on Twitter. Retweet their substance. (Ensure that it passes your channel and just offer it if you feel it is worth).
- ✓ Repeat the procedure on different systems like LinkedIn, Facebook, Quora, and so forth.

Day 81 – Automating sales operations

One of the keys to success in sales in software is the ability to focus on critical issues and activities relating to IT services and software. Tasks such as lead sustaining; searching, and contacting involve a ton of overhead work. You should invest some time to refresh contacts in the CRM, recording leads, and revising messages across domains. Since there are devices accessible that can enable you to upgrade your productivity and automate various heavily time consuming activities, it helps focus on preparing for the actual sales meetings and target achievement.

Checklist

- ✓ Use tools to craft email layouts that you can utilize and send them out at all times. Even though customizing and adding personal touch in each email to the beneficiary is important, it can be extremely useful and effective to have a premise of data and a plan that can be used readily and save a lot of time that is wasted in preparation of these.
- ✓ Create a layout for assignments like connecting with a prospect, booking a business meeting, and follow-up after a business meeting.
- ✓ Use tools to coordinate your Gmail and CRM. These can automatically create new leads and upgrade existing one in your CRM which eliminates the need for data-entry.

- ✓ Use various tools to automate any activity on Twitter and other social media while you focus on other equally important tasks during the day.

DAY 100- What next?

Now that you have managed to live by the first 100 day plan, you are equipped with a wealth of sales tactics and strategies. By this time, you have a better sense of your sales style, the practices that work best for you as well as the awareness about your apparent shortcomings. From this point on, you will continue to hone your skills while working on your limitations. Since you've been in software sales for over three months, you'll have a rather large amount of activities to reference. It is a good idea to go over your average sales rate, communication or meeting activity, and other significant metrics that may be used to evaluate your performance. Take a hard look at your performance in order to identify and fix your weak areas. For instance, if you make a lot of discovery calls but observe that most of your prospects tend to go silent after the interaction, the reason could be that you're unable to introduce a sense of urgency. Thus, it is a good idea to look back and evaluate your performance and work towards bettering self.

To make a compelling 100-day plan, we should know the company's area of interest. As a software sales professional, it is your duty to understand and compile a list of target areas and build connection on social media and elsewhere. Use opinions of clients, colleagues, your authority and self-thoughtfulness to build such a list. Once you realize that, you would then be able to make 30, 60, and 90 days quantifiable plans of how to enhance in those regions to achieve sales objectives. It winds up as a basis to continue estimating our advance as for the activity for each and every day. When you are finished with 100-day plan, you can comprehend the areas that you performed well and those that need change. Equipped with this extra information, make the next 100-day plan and repeat this cycle as an organized process.

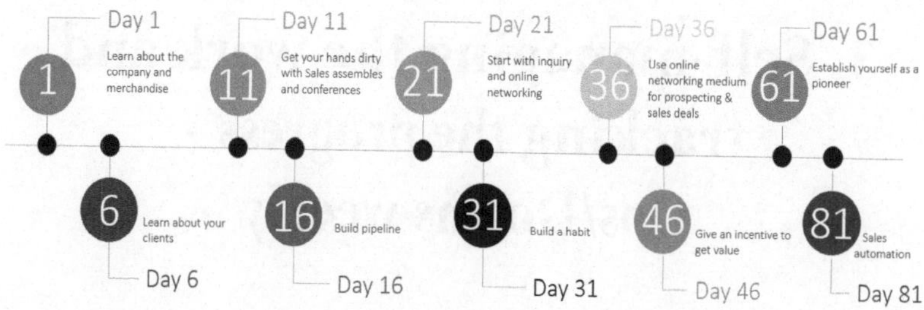

Figure 3 How to spend first 100 days at your job

3. Self-managing the work and tracking the progress - Ups/Downs weekly

"Ups and Downs captures emotional sense of organization"

– Ray August

When working in the sales domain, you confront many difficulties. One of them is dealing with the absence of "progress"; that feeling you get when you lose a customer, you don't get recognized for your diligent work or your competition is eating your piece of lunch in the overall industry. We have all been there! How we "handle" the result of any hardship is critical to build the stamina required to maintain a business in the long run.

It is an absolute necessity to keep positive outlook even amidst chaos and disadvantageous circumstances. This will help in focusing on the important aspects and building the business instead of lashing out on the negatives and losing hope. This chapter is dedicated to impart strategies on self-management and the importance of progress tracking which helps in keeping advancing when things take a downturn.

Self-management requires an interlocking set of structures and practices. Being able to self-manage can help you further your career goals in nearly any type of business or industry.

Employers appreciate self-starters who can get and stay motivated without constant supervision and prodding. You have a greater likelihood of getting prestigious accounts and projects because managers know you'll get the job done right with little or no oversight.

Self-management is mostly individual management, time management, and life management. It is taking charge of your life and steering it in the desired direction. As the old Confucian saying goes, "On the off chance that you don't change the street you're going on, you'll most likely wind up where you're going." Every aspiring person, at some in time, makes a firm choice about where he or she needed to go and after that found a way to arrive. What's more, you can do this for yourself as well.

We say things, for example, "I'm a sales representative", "I'm a manager", or "I work in such-and-such a business making such-and-such a showing with regards to". Since we have a tendency to wind up what we consider, the more we depict ourselves to others as being our main thing, the more we consider ourselves what we do. Maybe this is the reason individuals who are let go or laid off experience a time of stun and enthusiastic turmoil. It's as if they've been cut off from their characters. You may have had that experience.

The truth of the matter is that you're not what you do. Rather, you're a heap of assets. You have the mix of elements that makes you a one of a kind and striking individual, unique in relation to any other person who ever has lived or who will ever live. You've experienced a wide range of encounters, both positive and negative. You've had a formal education, and you've gained from the different jobs and exercises that you've done. You have an extraordinary knowledge, quite a bit of which isn't yet created to the full. You have abilities that you've gained through diligent work, lessons and practice.

You have capacities that you were conceived with, which make it simple for you to carry out specific employments and to achieve certain undertakings. You have energy, aspiration, objectives and opportunities. You have a theory of life, however created it is, and you have states of mind and points of view that make you remarkable. The federal government has distinguished in excess of 22,000 diverse occupation classifications; when you set up every one of your aptitudes together, you're most likely equipped for exceeding expectations at many jobs, doing distinctive things in various organizations and businesses.

As the clinician Abraham Maslow once stated, "The account of mankind is simply the tale of men and ladies undercutting themselves." The normal individual tends to make due with far not as much as he's able to do and after that marvels why he's so disappointed and baffled with his life. The truth of the matter is that you have an inherent drive toward the acknowledgment of your full limit. There's a power inside you that makes you fretful and discontent, and that drives you up and up toward the accomplishment you had always wanted and desired.

There are many ways of exceling in self-management. In the following section, there are a few things to remember while preparing for self-management in a software sales position:

Know Your Role

Understanding exactly what your role as a software sales professional entails can help you become a better self-manager. Become acquainted with every component of your job as a software sales person and make sure you constantly meet or surpass expectations. Request your managers for briefs about every major task you handle to ensure that you know the specifics of what you need to provide, both individually and in conjunction with colleagues. Interact with your manager and discuss the task in hand to avoid time loss due to processing in the wrong direction.

Be Organized

Being organized plays a major role in enabling one to be on-task and work efficiently. It will significantly help to develop a filing or categorizing system for storing information and creating charts in order to track growth in multiple areas. Sales meetings are the single most important aspect of your job and prepare well in advance for them. Never leave anything for the last minute, as it will cause stress and frustration eventually leading to poor performance and loss of client.

Prioritizing and Time Management

Sales is a job that requires one to have the ability to prioritize and understand which task requires immediate attention and in what degree. You need to prioritize activities and ensure that the most serious tasks are attended to, urgently. Drafting a daily "to do" lists can be helpful and anything that is not completed by the end of the day gets moved onto the following day's priority list. Allocate a certain amount of time on a regular basis for long-term projects.

Self-management is essentially about managing your time intelligently. Make the most of the time you spend at work by designating definite times to different tasks and responsibilities. Don't overcrowd your day and keep some spare time for unexpected events, meetings that might run late or tasks that need extra attention.

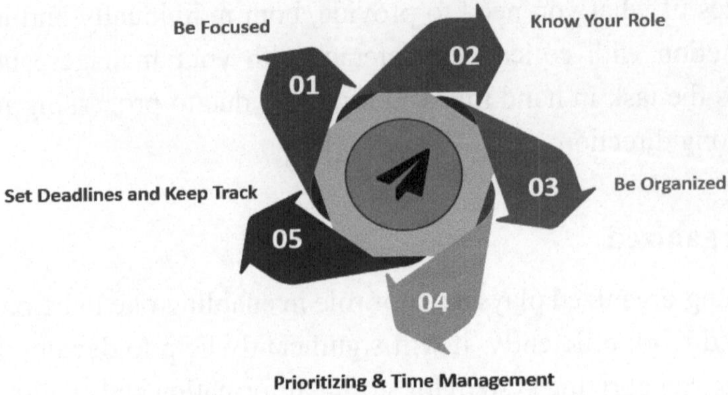

Fig: 4 – Ways to Excel at Self-Management

Set Deadlines and Keep Track

Self-dictate deadlines for yourself before they are set by the employer. It can help manage your time better and be more productive. This will not only permit you to complete your tasks in time but also give you time to review them for accuracy. This also means you won't be the reason for delay in team's performance.

Be Focused

Keep yourself motivated to finish the tasks on hand by ignoring distractions, practicing stress-reduction techniques and establishing attainable professional goals. Don't swing between different projects or spread yourself too thin by overscheduling your time or promising your services, when you cannot provide.

In order to develop self-managing sales professionals, managers need to inculcate various techniques that would promote the idea of self-management and independent progress tracking. Development Dimensions International, the

Association for Quality and Participation, and *Industry Week conducted a study in 1990 on the existing practices around self-managed teams. The study defined a self-directed team as*

> Members of self-directed teams typically handle job assignments, plan and schedule work, make production-related decisions, and take action on problems. Members of self-directed teams work with a minimum of direct supervision. As such, the teams are not quality circles or cross-functional task groups. ... These teams are characterized by:
>
> - Face-to-face interaction in natural work groups;
> - Responsibility for producing a definable product;
> - Responsibility for a set of interdependent tasks; and
> - Control over managing and executing tasks.

The sales cycle can be a long and complicated process. Some prospects take longer to close, while others convert quickly and easily. Some prospects may need a different kind of selling approach. If you are leading a team of sales professionals, you may find that at the other end of the spectrum, your sales staff also have different styles of functioning. Some of them may struggle with certain tasks. For others, there may be a specific point in the cycle where things go wrong and potential customers walk away. At every step in the sales cycle, you want to be able to keep track of information so that you can use it to improve your results. Creating and filling out sales reports is a great way to stay on top of everything that goes on in your cycle.

The value of sales reports

Sales reports give you access to invaluable data that is generated by your team as they work. Here are some of the basic things you can uncover from a sales report:

- Who your customers are;
- Where your leads are coming from;
- What prompts prospects to buy;
- What keeps prospects from buying;
- Campaign success rate;
- Closing rate

Keeping track

In order for a sales manager to track how much time is spent on different sales activities, and measuring the effectiveness of the sales team, it makes sense to look into the daily activities of each sales representative as they interact with clients and prospects. These reports give you a picture of how many leads have been touched in a day and how many prospects have been spoken to. Some prospects are easy to pin down, others may need frequent reminders and calls. Depending on the nature of the prospect and how much cajoling they need, you can check on the frequency of calls and follow-ups. You can also get an idea as to the nature of these calls, the outcome, and the average length of each call.

In order to tackle your sales progress, it is advisable to invest in a good sales tracking tool. A sales tracking tool is a way of documenting the interactions a lead has with your business, right from the point of entry, emails and phone calls that they receive, and how they move down your funnel, to ultimately become your customer. This process, also called sales tracking allows you to get a visual idea of how a lead is conversing with you and any pain points that may be present in your sales cycle. It also helps you understand the effectiveness of your sales funnel.

So how to set up a sales tracking process?

Stage 1: Identify your intended interest group of software users

Similar to the standard with most sales and promoting firms, you need to know who your client is. This will enable you to design out the rest of your procedure with substantially more lucidity. Know who might be the influencers, leaders and purchasers for what you offer.

Stage 2: Identify your sources

Next, you have to know the stages that this gathering of people would be available in, both on the web and in person. Make sense of which online networking stages they would visit the most, which catchphrases they scan for, and what sites they visit. On the off chance that you have an application, you can attempt in-application promotions also. You would now be able to get a more robust view of them.

Stage 3: Allocate stages for each lead

Characterize and organize where your lead could fall into. This could be something like cold lead, prospect, warm lead, hot lead, and client. The stages would fluctuate over organizations and ventures. You would then be able to perceive easily where in the business pipeline a lead is at any given time.

Stage 4: Define the ways in which your lead can connect with you

You have to recognize the manners by which you mean to support your leads. This could be through email marketing, trickle showcasing, online courses, e-books or more. Understand every type of correspondence and the impact it has on your leads. This could be through online networking, talk, web structures, e-mail and via telephone. This progression guarantees that you can monitor what sustaining exercises are helping a prompt change over.

Stage 5: Set up metrics that would need to be measured consistently

Since you have the framework set up, the last stage advancement would comprehend what you ought to gauge with the business following framework. Is it the measure of activity your site gets? Or then again the quantity of individuals who roll in from one specific source? Or on the other hand the normal time it takes for a lead to turn into a client. You would then be able to make reports in view of your prerequisites to make the most out of your business.

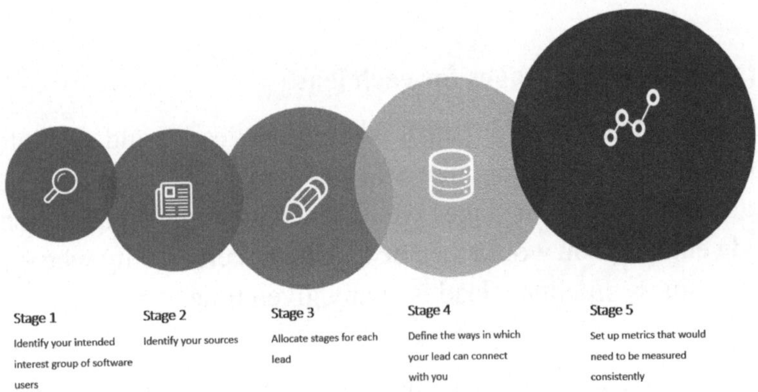

Figure 5 Different stages in setting up a sales tracking process.

Essential metrics that need to be measured:

You have effectively set up the process. Then, one needs to investigate in detail the final step in the process. Your business understanding doesn't simply stop with knowing how the lead interfaces with you. It also includes its impact on your business and its income. For decent sales, following procedure should enable you to gather these measurements

- **Sale per source:** Calculate the quantity of offers that occur through your different lead sources. This encourages you discover which lead sources are giving you the most extreme measure of business. This encourages you to focus your deals and advertising or promotional endeavors more on those channels.
- **Total sale in a set time period:** Calculate the quantity of offers that have occurred on a month-to-month, quarterly or yearly premise. This gives the management a perspective of how the business is performing overall.
- **Sale per demography:** This could reveal to you what number of clients rolls in from a specific age gathering, work profile, or topography. This encourages you to make sense of who your optimal purchaser persona is and you can target them better with paid crusades and in addition through advertising.
- **Sale per sales person:** Know which sales person is acquiring the most extreme measure of income. You can utilize this as an execution screen as well as an inspiration to keep the spirit of your business teams collaborate.
- **Average time to close a deal:** This metric encourages you to figure to what extent it takes for a lead to convert into a client. For a few organizations, particularly B2C the business cycle is considerably shorter contrasted with

B2B organizations. By making sense of this, you can set ideal and achievable focuses for your business group.

- **New versus repeating client sales:** This metric tells you how much business is originating from new clients and how much from more seasoned ones. You can likewise make sense of the amount it expenses to get another client, contrasted with the amount it expenses to hold an old one.
- **Churn rate:** Know the rate at which clients are leaving your business and why. You would then be able to attempt to restore lost clients and get them back or endeavor to keep similar oversights from happening once more.
- **Average income per client:** Know how much income every client is bringing you. This will enable you to adjust your intended interest group too. You would realize that too lucrative or too low paying leads would not fit your business.

Advantages of Sales tracking

Here is a list of the substantial and impalpable advantages that you get from executing a business following process for your firm:

- In-depth insight into your sales channel.
- Ability to monitor the effectiveness of your team and perform quality checks when necessary.
- Better knowledge about which software products help acquire the highest income and why
- Opportunity to learn when something turns out badly and avoid unnecessary risks.
- Better correspondence with your interest group of prospects or clients by observing their conduct.

- Increase in consumer loyalty by tending to their needs and expectations, and giving personalized solutions to them.

The goal of this chapter was to discuss the need for self-management and tracking progress of sales in the software industry. As a sales professional, one has a lot of tasks in hand whether that is approaching new clients, learning deeply about the software to sell, building contacts or preparing sales pitch and attending meetings. Due to the nature of the job, it is essential that the sales professional understands the need for self-management and keeping a track of progress made during any specific period. A habit of making a weekly progress report will help software sales professionals to not only keep themselves updated about their progress but understand the software sales status at the time. Competent sales professionals always make the habit of adopting techniques and acquire skills for self-management and tracking progress.

4. Working with the Single source of truth - SugarCRM

"Any watched number will improve" – Dr. Raghu Korrapati

A Single source of truth is a single point of access and modification for Data element. It requires both a standardized information model and incorporation with the end goal that makers and customers of an information component all enter single source of data. Single wellspring of truth is a design practice and information methodology that guarantees that information is solid, exact and secured. There are many software products available in the market to manage customer relationship. One great example is SugarCRM which is also the world's largest open source CRM. It engages associations to pick up and hold clients by giving more noteworthy productivity and control over their business pipeline. As an open-stage online CRM arrangement, Sugar is effortlessly adaptable to meet an association's evolving needs. It offers an upper hand by furnishing associations with a 360-degree perspective of their clients.

CRMs when all is said and done empower organizations to make better associations with their clients by social occasion information on the chronicled connections and clients' practices. By associating your SugarCRM to dateline, you will have the capacity to investigate your CRM information next to each other with back orders, deals, promoting, or some other information source that you likewise associated and so on. You will also be able to have more precise bits of knowledge on your execution. You at that point have an outline of your whole business in one place, and thus settle on better educated choices that will enable it to develop.

Numerous organizations have seen issues of information discontinuity: information that is copied in numerous spots, frequently refreshed on an easygoing premise, and with little clarity and more duplicates. This information could be anything from software product catalog, through to client contact data or retail deals figures or software sales. Following are some of the key challenges stemming from the lack of single source of truth and how it affects the success of sales professionals and the organization.

Work flow slows down

Very frequently we see that individuals' everyday work process is backed off by not having certain access to business information. We find that time is frequently spent (or wasted) in checking with others about the legitimacy of a specific dataset: invariably requiring the sales professional to sit tight for a reaction which may push them back in their sales effort by hours or days.

Decision-making skills are impaired

Associations ought to drive their basic leadership by utilizing as much information as is accessible. Where there is vulnerability with regards to the legitimacy of information, associations are frequently unfit to answer what ought to be generally insignificant, however vital, inquiries. For example, "How many user licenses of say insurance policy admin software did we offer in the Americas in February 2018?" or

"How many clients did not renew their license or subscription of fraud detection software because of value issues in the second quarter 2018?"

At the point when these straightforward inquiries aren't effortlessly made available, we normally find that the sales professionals are not able, to utilize information to settle on powerful choices.

Capacity to innovate is reduced

The sales organization that experiences information discontinuity frequently finds that their capacity to advance and actualize new frameworks is hindered. It will not be able to leverage any new CRM that has more exciting capabilities and enables to stay ahead of the competition, if it does not have a good control of customer data. It is because without such control, the sales organization would not know where to host customer data, how to analyze customer experience through various channels and so on.

Individuals invest excess energy in duplicating data

While not generally the situation, the manifestations already point by point indicate that individuals are investing a lot of their energy performing manual and mistake inclined duplication of information. Each time some individual physically inputs information is another open door for making errors. Also, it's not the effective use of employees' time, both from a cost and motivational viewpoint.

All alone and consolidated, these difficulties over and over again put organizations off guard, gradually chipping away at the edges of operational effectiveness.

With the expanding selection of (or the re-naming of existing activities as) "big data", the significance of information trustworthiness and an organization's capacity to dig this information for knowledge turns out to be perpetually obvious. By overlooking, or working around the single source of truth challenges in your company, you're likely to lose competitive edge...

At any rate, characterizing which duplicate of information - on the off chance that you totally should have information exist in more than one place - is the "Master", and implementing automated procedures as much as possible when replicating the data across various data stores,, a sales organization will be able to make genuine progress in its efforts to improve sales effectiveness by mining the data and making data-driven decisions.

Data Realities

Single source of information is a solid solution that requires information be refreshed and gotten to from one place with no duplicates skimming around. By and by, expansive associations locate this hard to actualize. For instance, numerous business off-the-rack items and cloud administrations have restrictive information models that are hard to change.

It is basic for structures to adopt a pragmatic strategy that doesn't entirely fit in with a single abundance of truth. ACE data management is one such approach that takes into consideration numerous duplicates and forms of information with a solitary access point utilizing methods, for example, information virtualization.

For advertisers searching for precise and noteworthy information, the attribution arrangement is the single wellspring of truth. Since a successful attribution arrangement does the accompanying things, advertisers can be positive about it as the single wellspring of truth:

1. It coordinates with promoting channels through API or UTM parameters to source unique information.
2. It coordinates with promoting mechanization and the CRM to associate the center and base of-the-channel information, including client transformation and income information.
3. It's multi-touch and creases all the promoting channels (both on the web and offline) into the same unified attribution display, which dispenses with two-fold including and channel inclination.
4. Attribution reports utilize a predictable lead, opportunity, and client definition, with the goal that a solitary individual or record's way can be taken after from first touch to client close and everything in-between.
5. Combining the greater part of the past focuses, it associates unique showcasing channel information to income information, with the goal that advertisers can see their effect on the primary concern.

At the point when advertisers have a shrewd attribution arrangement, they know where to go for conclusive promoting information. Instead of guessing which advertising channel actually drove the 10 clients in the speculative manner, an attribution arrangement would have demonstrated that possibly Facebook represented 30% of the 10 clients' voyages, while AdWords represented the other 70%. The advertiser could then make a move in view of that and reallocate a larger amount of the monetary allowance to AdWords. The leap forward effect of this analysis is opened up when there are many promoting channels and several campaigns.

Never again do advertisers need to wind up confounded, baffled, and deadened by numerous, opposing sources of information. At the point when there is a single repository of truth that acquires every one of the information and treats it with precision and reasonableness, advertisers can settle on savvy choices with certainty

It is a routine with regards to organizing data models and related database mapping to such an extent that each datum component is put away precisely once. This is an attempted and tried model with its standards touching relatively every application. Enterprise Resources Planning (ERP) frameworks are based over this standard with center information like clients, items, financials dwelling in one place, with this information being accessible to outside frameworks like online sales frameworks, purpose of offers, communication, business knowledge, and so on.

Take a straightforward case of items being accessible online for a standard web store. The ERP framework may have business leads around item satisfaction, terms for a client, restock levels and substantially more. The online store presents data on what levels of stock are accessible to offer a thing, decrements the thing from the ERP item framework. The ERP framework can shoot business controls around restocking. This permits the ERP frameworks' business standards to be utilized by the Point of Sale framework in nearly a similar design.

When conversing with clients, numerous tell about their cloud based CRM frameworks, Point of Sale frameworks, Project following framework and I ponder, "Where is the ERP framework?"

Gartner's current production on 'Taming the Digital Dragon' states it well:

> "The center of big business IT foundation, applications, for example, ERP, data and sourcing has worked for the IT in past and should be redesigned for the computerized future. The redesigns incorporate moving to an all the more

> approximately coupled 'postmodern-ERP' worldview, sending open and private mists, making the data engineering and abilities to abuse enormous information, and enlarging traditional sourcing with more development, including sourcing from, and collaborating with, littler and less develop ventures."

Cloud based frameworks are digging in for the long haul in this advanced time. A significant number of the executions have cover of others framework, stock, financials. For instance, Lightspeed which at its center is a POS framework, additionally has a lite form of a client framework, stock framework, financials and an online trade framework. The information for clients and financials needs to exist for Lightspeed to have a reasonable POS advertising. Analyze the client record highlight in this POS framework with Salesforce, the decision of Salesforce is a straightforward one.

When incorporating these frameworks, every framework converses with the other framework over API. Full scale mixes utilize multi-ace replication crosswise over frameworks, implies a change to stock levels are repeated to different frameworks where this data is required and the other way around. In some cases it is faulty if the business controls around a substance are shot when refreshes are made over API. Issues in this setup go from business rules not functioning correctly in the essential framework, synchronization issues, superseding of urgent data because of synchronization issues and others. The opposite end of this range is no replication of information crosswise over frameworks. Individuals work with Excel spreadsheets and refresh stock, client information crosswise over frameworks. The issues that accompanies both these kind of setups run from – sat around idly, frameworks obsolete, weariness and lost time.

The design behind Single Source of Truth (SSOT) idea has been around for a very long time. The adjustment in deduction needs to go from a table to a particular framework that is the expert for that arrangement of data for your undertaking. Which framework is your arrangement of record for your key business frameworks? How is this information expended and can the business decisions be held in that one framework while refreshes happen on different frameworks? With this computerized period and a move from one focal ERP framework, and development of numerous frameworks with covering informational collections issues compound when this principle of Single Source of Truth is damaged. Try not to be an Eve where your Single Source of Truth is lost.

5. Completing Trip reports and owning the closure of action items

A significant part of sales involves completing trip reports and owning the closure of action items. These two aspects of sales professional will enable them to evaluate their interaction with various potential clients. Each trip requires a complete account of various elements relating to that trip. Writing a comprehensive business trip report requires the willingness to capture all pertinent information about the customer's requirement, needs and concerns and to make sure the trip report is submitted the same day to your manager or relevant office that manages sales operations. This chapter is designed to provide an insight into writing a trip report and owning the closure of action items in a software sale.

It is a common question among budding sales professionals, how vital is it to complete a business trip report the very same day as the client visit? All things considered, since preserving client data is fundamental to winning business, it is fair to assume that finishing that business trip report that day is central to the sales progress. It is absolutely essential to ensure that the most important data is documented and sent to sales manager or sales operations manager. The information gathered during these trips will be used later for various purposes; one of them would be to devise a sales pitch. Thus, this data must be retained in easily consumable and well organized form. Since, human mind is not capable of retaining too much data, a sales professional should use the following tips to record the most data:

1. **Write down Information in Front of Client:** During client visits, there will certainly be times when you'll have the ability to record all relevant data about the client's necessities, concerns and expectations. But this is often only possible if you've requested that opportunity earlier. In this way, before going to meet the client, request to meet with them in an informal setting so that thoughts can be exchanged freely. Your client ought to be more than willing to enable you to record all the data you require because it is your job to acquire all the information necessary to know what and how they want.
2. **Use a "Pre-characterized" Code:** There will be those circumstances where you just won't have the capacity to compose everything down. Regardless of whether you've considered that time alone with the client, there will in any case be times when you won't have an opportunity to catch essential data. An answer is to think of a pre-characterized code or terminology that assigns particular code to the data relevant to your market. The code could be basic letters and numbers that assign data about the competition, opportunity size such as number of user licenses or subscriptions, winning price, and so on. At the point when those circumstances won't enable you to compose everything down, utilize your own pre-characterized codes.
3. **Document Preliminary Thoughts about the Visit:** Immediately after your client visit, set aside some time to record your underlying considerations so as to catch them inside your business trip report. There are dependably those unobtrusive clues and events amid the client visit

that various sales personnel either disregard, or can't catch. Be straightforward in your evaluation about how the visit went. Record your considerations about the state of mind of the visit, the client's body language, the personality of the client team and the general state of their business. In every client visit, there are critical snippets of data that must be caught.

4. **Categorize Information In The Business Trip Report:** Simply recording snippets of data is no real way to compose a sales trip report. The data must be clear, compact and exhibited in a way that permits everybody to understand and share the data in similar manner. Similarly, make sure to isolate the data inside the sales trip report. You could do it by business openings, client needs and concerns, and general notes about competition and industry trends. Most sales experts question why their trip report for a forthcoming client needs to be done and submitted to the manager around the same time. Basically, ability to remember events that happened during the client visit is key to guaranteeing that all the related data is gathered. The more time is lost before the sales trip report is initiated, the more likely to miss out data about a critical need, or concern or expectation of the client. It's human instinct to overlook and individuals have a tendency to overlook vital data which is not recorded. While a few sales experts have solid memory retention, others must work at holding key snippets of data.

Most companies require employees to write sales trip report after every trip. It is good business practice to write a summary of every trip. There is no single right way to write sales trip report. Sales trip reports are though usually organized as document, which states the purpose of the trip, location of the trip, personnel interacted, what you learned, what suggestions you have to offer and what is the course of action that will be taken etc. It is recommended to keep notes throughout your trip and prepare the report as soon as possible i.e. while the details are still fresh in your mind.

What details to be included in a trip report?

A trip report is organized as memorandum for managers or sales leaders within your sales team.

1. Start by filling out basic information like details with regard to the names, location and the date of report.
2. Disclose information relating to the sales trip i.e. where, when and why. Key aspects of the trip must be highlighted like what was the purpose of the trip and when did it take place.
3. Provide a short description of the trip. The description must include the reason for your trip. For example, as a software sales professional, the purpose of your trip could be "visiting potential customers" or "making a sales pitch to new businesses". The description should provide some insight, for instance, "visiting businesses with software contracts expiring within the next 6 months" or "attending the quarterly customer reception in the west zone".
4. Summarize key aspects of your trip. On the basis of the purpose of your trip, provide a comprehensive analysis of the key points during the trip.
5. Include information about the person you met, the purpose of the meeting and the final outcome.
6. Highlight solid outcomes with conclusions or recommendations. For example, if you "succeeded in

renewing 80% of all contracts concluding within the next 6 months", it can be needs to be recorded for various purposes.

7. Emphasize on any follow up actions required from your sales trip. For example, if you need to "visit the company again in the next couple of months in order to work on the remaining clients with expiring contracts", then it should be brought to light in this report.
8. Make sure to clearly state all follow up actions i.e. what exactly needs to be done, who will be in charge of doing it and by when must it be done.

These steps will assist in creating a good report where all queries and concerns related to a sales trip are answered and available for others in the team or the company to use.

Follow up diligently on action items from trip report

An action item is a specific piece of work that needs follow-up and execution. Some examples of action items include transferring particular data to somebody, orchestrating a meeting, and giving a quick estimate on a bit of work. There are two common methods used to oversee action items. For all non-trivial action items, the best-suited approach is to include the items as exercises in the project work plan. You assign resources and an end date and then direct the activity and track it just like an ordinary activity. This is the better way to tackle as it keeps the work exercises in a single place and enables the project administrator to see the schedule impact of assigning action items to team colleagues. In the event that colleagues are allotted action items that take significant effort, it can negatively affect their assigned work.

Another famous approach is to track and oversee activity things on a different Action Item Log. A different Action Item Log just bodes well if the work exercises involve maybe a couple hours of effort. If it is substantially more than that, you need to put the action item in the work plan. Action items are ordinarily time sensitive. In the event that an action item has not been finished in a sensible time period, it ought to be shut and wiped out. Action items are now and then mistakenly mixed in with issues. An action item ought not to be mistaken for an issue. An issue is a concern that will detrimentally affect the project if left uncertain. An action item is essentially some subsequent work that should be performed.

In the event that you include an action item into the work plan, you'll track them just like any work plan action. In the event that you record smaller action item in an Action Item Log, you can utilize the following procedure to oversee them.

1. The project manager enters the action item in the Action Item Log. This records its reality to guarantee that it gets consideration and is completed.
2. The task supervisor allocates the action item to a colleague who accepts accountability for the action item and makes the essential strides to finish it. The undertaking administrator might be relegated action item too.
3. A date for the completion of each action item must be entered in the log, alongside an estimate of the amount of effort required.
4. If completing an action item includes more work than planned or estimated, it should be conveyed to the project manager so it can be added to the work plan.
5. The Action Item Log needs to be inspected regularly to guarantee that action item have been finished effectively. Since things in the Action Item Log take just a single or two hours, you should anticipate finishing them fairly quickly.
6. The project manager ensures those action items are completed in time.

Action items might be small, however they should still be tracked and finished. Here are some great approaches to compose better action items:

1. Keep in mind that the "capture stage" is not quite the same as the "process stage".

Regardless of whether you utilize a formalized profitability framework like GTD (Getting Things Done) or a more instinctive, home-developed method for getting stuff out of your head, there are two discrete stages: capture and process. "Catch" is the place you get matter out of your head, and "process" is the place you really break down what you have gotten out of your thoughts. This qualification is much similar to the refinement amongst drafting and editing; the fundamental objective of the catch is to get it so you can see it, and the process stage is required so you can comprehend it. The things underneath are about what you do amid the process stage after you've gotten your things caught.

2. Compose each action item as though you were composing it to another person.

Action items are frequently shorthand codes for us and are implied just to refresh our memory. While this may work for things we may need to do today, what frequently happens is that an assignment we intend to do today gets booted into what's to come. It is quite possible that the individual who peruses the action item two months from now is not you but someone else who may not understand what that shorthand code implied. I've discovered that when individuals compose the items as though they were thinking of them to another person, they keep in touch with them the correct way. That implies their lives are less demanding later on when they get to those action items they don't need to complete a cluster of speculating about what should be finished.

3. Incorporate the "when" in the action item assignment.

Help yourself out by ensuring that the action items contain their due dates. This helps you to build up the act of promptly having the capacity to recognize what should be finished by a certain time versus what should be finished when time permits. Likewise, consider recognizing when something is expected by another person and how early you need it finished. For instance: a simple "TPS Report" could now be "Draft TPS Report by Tuesday (due to the manager by Wednesday)."

4. Assign out ownership for the action item in team environments, always

This one can be ambiguous, on the grounds that occasionally it's not clear who needs to complete an item and you can make them in charge of it. Be that as it may, sometimes, you'll have to allocate ownership just with the goal to complete it. Remember that if you do not assign a specific owner to the action item, then by default you will be responsible to get it done! **Be clear about relay action items.**

Many action item are intended to spur the activity of someone else in the chain of projects; think about a multi-people task as a multi stage sprint, wherein one individual runs a bit of the race and hands off the baton to the next. A lot of time is often lost due to poor handoffs. When taking care of transfers, you can either part the things into two discrete things — e.g., "Create software comparison report for Client X by Tuesday" and "Send reviewed comparison report to Client X by Friday" — or build up the inward habit of consequently sending the items to the next individual in the chain. Well-working groups with successful individuals usually rely on the latter since they believe in each other and the process.

5. Give context as a remark or note.

Giving the background information about the assignment —, for example, expressing why the product comparison report is important— can help you and whoever gets the task, finish it better, and frequently inspires the individual to do it. An entire chunk of tasks can appear as busywork, yet knowing where and why your work fits in can be unbelievably useful. You'd be astonished how much taking an additional minute or two to compose several sentences can influence the quality and swiftness of execution. These steps are recorded in a consistent, successive order that'll enable you to process each action item. You'll see that the order moves from "What should be done?" to "by when?" to "by whom?" to "what next?" to "why?", Many solopreneurs experience difficulty in assigning tasks or action items to others because they naturally think that everything that should be done should be completed by them.

6. Practice Composing Better Action Items

Most things that are worth doing take time and practice; and composing better action items is no different. These things are habits, which are acquired by making sense of what works and what doesn't. It obviously requires a lot of time and significant energy. Be that as it may, considerably more time is typically wasted by ineffectively planning action item since they're not inspiring or driving the activities needed to finish them.

As a software sales professional, following these steps to take and complete action items can help you to excel. Owning the closure of action items as well as writing sales report will help understand and work on sales strategies in the future. Just like any other practice, it'll in the long run turn into a regular habit. Completing things takes much less time to finish when they become a habit like these because it's one less thing you need to consider and work on. Incorporating such practices into day-to-day sales protocol can have a positive impact on sales professionals.

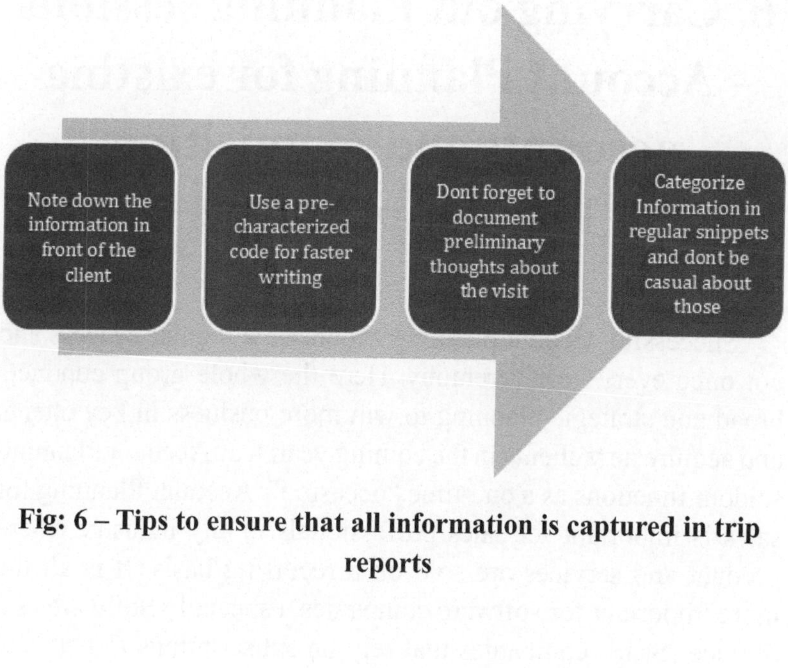

Fig: 6 – Tips to ensure that all information is captured in trip reports

6. Carrying out Planning sessions - Account Planning for existing accounts and Acquisition Plan for prospects

Successful account planning should be a regular process and not once every year ceremony. Here the whole group conducts broad and strategic planning to win more business in key clients and acquire new clients in the coming year. Key Account Planning seldom functions as a one-time "occasion". Account Planning for sales is important for sales professionals in any industry where product and services are sold on a recurring basis. It is all the more important for software companies, especially Software as a Service (SaaS) companies that rely on subscriptions to generate their revenue. Every account absolutely matters, specifically the enterprise accounts, which typically contribute the largest pie of the recurring revenue.

According to a survey conducted by CSO Insights in 2016, with the random approach of leaving account planning up to each salesperson, win rates decreased to 42.9%, compared to the average win rate for forecast deals of the study of 46.2%. It's a difference of 3.3 percentage points, and a decline of 7.7%. Reflect on what such difference in the increase in the number of deals won would mean for your organization!

Progressing account planning gives advantages to you, the business head, and your whole Sales group.

Progressing account planning isn't simply intended to profit you the business head yet rather gives advantages to everybody when effectively executed. For the sales professional ongoing account planning encourages them compose (and organize) their domain, recognize objectives for their clients, and distinguish their offerings accordingly. Powerful regional account planning additionally encourages them to concentrate their endeavors on the best and most achievable open doors that exist. It also helps them to convey to other colleagues what they need them to assist for achieving this ambitious plan.

For you the business head, progressing account planning makes you to rapidly pick up a comprehension of a sales professional's objectives, approaches to achieve those objectives, and strategic plans to deliver best results. Composed designs additionally help you as the mentor to search for holes or unfulfilled open doors inside their account plans so you can give instructing counsel and help to the colleagues.

As the pioneer of your business group, you have the chance to mentor and inspire every one of the colleagues. What is the extent of making progress in your team's account planning have you been driving to finish and take forward for actions?

Account planning can expand your upper hand.

Fruitful and progressing account planning can expand your group's upper hand and offering adequacy by helping them distinguish, sort out, and create composed ventured plans of what they need to do to win a client's business.

Once built up, you can utilize these composed plans for advanced training of your team, and you can also use it to convey the requirement for extra assistance from different divisions and managers inside your organization. After a deal is won or lost, use these account plans to mentor the sales professionals on what worked well and what changes are needed to improve success rates in closing new business.

Yet, numerous account planning sessions cover the wrong "stuff". Most account and regional sales planning overlook the proactive "future centered" offering endeavors that can really expand your group's upper hand. They just concentrate on wanting to recognize for an account the quantity of calls they intend to make on that client and to distinguish any booked unique occasions or courses of events for these client accounts.

Leading your sales group through ongoing account planning.

Intrigued by expanding your group's account planning endeavors? Successful account planning is best actualized when the accompanying six key thoughts are started and kept up:

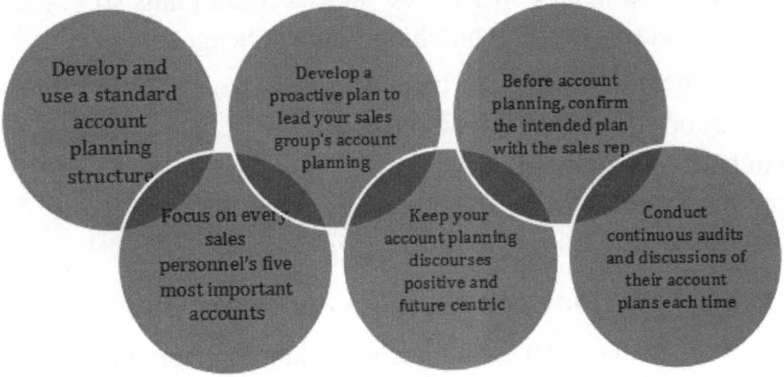

Fig: 7 – Key thoughts while performing account planning for sales

1. Develop and use a standard account planning structure.

One of the key tools in driving powerful account planning

is to create and use a standard account planning structure. A vital part of an effective account planning is institutionalization and consistency of the process and documents used across the team for an activity. In spite of the fact that every last account plan could be distinctive in the objectives or usage designs distinguished, the planning devices and steps you take after it, should be reliable. With everybody following and utilizing a similar planning structure and process, you, as their mentor and pioneer would now be able to understand predictable deals and offer recommendations to win those deals.

An example of Client Account Planning for Sales Template is incorporated toward the end of this book. This is a framework I have created and executed for some of my customers. I am glad to have you alter and additionally adjust this template to fit your software and services offering situations and business culture in your geography. You simply need all your colleagues follow the structure once it's concluded as a standard.

Section I concentrates on providing executive level summary on "Where we are currently" leading to Section II to discuss "Where we need to go/grow" and "how do we intend to get there" in terms of growing business with this account.

As you conduct the Account Planning sessions in a cadence, review the effectiveness of the plan in terms of achieving the desired results and keep it updated to continue to develop and grow the Client account's business throughout the year and beyond.

2. Concentrate on every sales person's five most important accounts.

Once you have standardized the account planning template and process across your sales team, next important action is to concentrate on every sales person's best five accounts. Make the account planning as compelling by co-developing it with your organization. Otherwise the account planning efforts will come up short in the event you ask your sales persons to finish account plans for all their "named accounts" as their first endeavor at account planning. Doing it alone, will likely reduce the success rate of your account planning efforts.

The most ideal approach to begin a group's account planning process is to build it point by point for their best or most essential five clients. Concentrating on their best five clients allows everyone time to figure out how to direct account planning efforts. It will give you, the sales manager, an opportunity to fortify your capabilities to effectively lead and mentor your team during account planning sessions. As your team gets better at such process, you can simply expand the number of client accounts that need a comprehensive account planning and subsequent actions to successfully execute them and win more business.

3. Develop a proactive plan to lead your sales group's account planning execution.

Now that you have standardized on account templates and completed them for the top five accounts for your sales team, next important step is to build up a proactive training plan to execute the actions documented in the plan. Take it with you when meeting with your group for account planning sessions. A regular cadence of account planning sessions will continue to happen as long as you, their business supervisor and pioneer, push it. When you quit getting information or status or blockers about your sales team's account plans, they'll quit creating or following any developed plans.

It is imperative to start off at the earliest by instructing and driving your group in the improvement of their top most client account(s) business. You should think about leading a group meeting in the presence of sales professionals as you demonstrate to them generally accepted methods to build up an account plan for a key client. Clearly walking your whole group through the advancement of a deal that you created for winning a key client's business can enable your colleagues to better comprehend what you're anticipating from any plan developed by them. Once you've demonstrated to them what you expect, you would then enable your sales team to finish this same procedure for their five biggest or most imperative client accounts.

Next meet "one-on-one", whether face to face or by phone with every sales person in your team to explore each deal in their five top most client account plans. This will give you a great deal of value to enable you to mentor and lead your sales person in considering and preparing their offering endeavors. You'll send a significant message to your colleagues if each time they discuss an important client account, you quickly add value to their developed plan. Likewise, raise any of these plans at whatever point you spend time with, or invest a lot of energy with, to any of your sales team.

As your sales professionals see you referencing and using their client specific account plans each time you talk about that client, you'll rapidly reinforce that these client account planning elements are a normal part of their activity and they will be more comfortable to accept your assistance or guidance. Finally, you need to reference and talk about any client account plan when there is conclusion to a deal whether it is a win or not. Once a client has agreed to give the business to your sales team, you need to take a step back and review the account plan and its execution with a specific focus on knowing which parts of it could have been enhanced or have been more complete and thus contributing to a win. This knowledge will expand the chances of winning next time, or if nothing else improve the effectiveness of sales pitching process more proficient as well as powerful for any future offering endeavors.

4. Keep your account planning discourses positive and future centric

As you build the momentum in institutionalizing the account plans and winning some business deals, you can look forward to effectively reinforce your group's account planning process by keeping the discussions positive and "future centered". Effective account planning occurs when it is directed in a positive and open condition. Your sales team will quit taking an interest and will keep away from any planning activity when they sense that such activity is a negative examination or isn't viewed as being of assistance and incentive to them.

Remind all in training sessions that this is a positive instructing session intended to help them to be more effective and for others to better see how they can bolster the offering endeavors of the sales team. Any issues or general sales execution rejections should be dealt with at another meeting and time. This isn't a gathering for you to be a "Military trainer" or to pound them!

You additionally need to work to keep your account planning meetings "strategic" and "vital" versus being impeded in "operational" elements. You should be more inspired by helping them build up a number of account plans with more creative deal structuring than to examine in detail how a particular client deal or meeting will advance. They will be taken care of later, far from this planning session. Keep more alignment to the master plan of where your sales team intends to run with a client and how they intend to arrive. The minute elements of what should be said and how it should be conveyed can be dealt with later as the individual advances materialize You additionally need these kinds of "bigger picture" sessions to stay more "future centered" rather than just fixating on earlier history issues or current domain issues.

A straightforward method to guarantee these gatherings stay positive and of incentive to your business colleagues is to clearly and explicitly ask, "Is this session helping?" toward the end of any account planning or sales training session. An affirmative response from your team will be a good indicator for a better performance as they see it as an incentive.

Always focus on 'How it can be done' than continue harping on challenges & negatives. "Keeping the positive spirit always" – is the key to success.

5. Before any account planning, confirm with your sales team the intended plan and general objectives of the session.

Next, it is time to reinforce your group's account planning process. Decreasing shocks to your sales team is an excellent way to bring down their resistance to your account planning efforts and an incredible method to keep them cheerful and engaged. You need to clearly explain ahead of time to your team what client accounts you need them to talk about in detail, what accounts they'd additionally get a kick out of the chance to examine, and the normal planning session beginning and completion times. Strictly adhere to the allotted time for these sessions.

Ensure that there is a motivational speech by an industry-renowned expert during an account planning session. It is a sign of success to your planning efforts if your sales team does the dominant part of talking and you just moderate and guide the team through your questions to the presenter. Keep in mind, any sales person finishing an account plan needs to feel it's their plan and they must own it or there will be little use for account planning efforts.

6. Conduct continuous reviews and discussions of their account plans each time you interact with your sales team.

Last but not least, keep on conducting progress surveys and information exchanges of any targeted account plans each time you meet or travel with one of your sales team members. The main objective is to get your business colleagues to see how much weight you're setting on these plans and to perceive how regularly you review or get some updates on the plan and actions you have put together. The more they see you referencing and getting updates or sharing your thoughts to advance the deals in their key client accounts, the more likely they'll help your account planning efforts and to contribute to the overall success of the sales unit.

It is thus important to understand account planning. Here are additional insights in order to make strategic account planning significant:

- **Clients are priority**: Begin with understanding of the whole setting in the client account, (for example, their business challenges, their budgetary execution, their business methodologies and plans pushing ahead, and so on.) and in their industry.
- **Examine the present state**: This incorporates existing business, consumer loyalty and issues, and revenue related execution. Break down the issues that you currently enable clients to resolve, and the benefits you have helped the client actualize so far. Map out your present relationship, the nature of the relationship, and how they acted in the relationship process so far. Characterize every vital activity to build up your current connections. At that point, identify where are your relationship holes? Who are the officials you don't approach at the present time? Creating associations with

them must be your key core interests. To do that, you'll need clear value propositions with crisp messages, and fantastic plans to drive their execution and enable them to accomplish their objectives. That is the reason the following two stages are key for progress.

- **Design and strategize a shared account planning technique**: This is frequently disregarded, or just diminished to "This year, I need to offer them X, and one year from now I need to offer them Y." This isn't a common account planning; this is an item push approach that doesn't work any longer. An effective account planning starts with the client's objectives and closures with how you can help them to accomplish these objectives, while guaranteeing in parallel that this technique is important for your company too.
- **Design and strategize creative account leads in order to acquire new business**: Now is an ideal opportunity to assemble every one of the pieces and to conceptualize to make new account leads. In any case, don't do this by itself. Welcome your offering and planning teams, your industry specialists, and kindly bear in mind your management team that regularly invests more energy with the clients than your account team ever will. Offer all the work you have done on the account plan with them before the meeting to generate new ideas. Capture all thoughts, delineate to the relationship, and characterize the important activities to propel the leads.
- **Understand the significance of horizontal growth potentials**: Where would you be able to leverage the success that you have helped the client realize? In another

specialty unit, in another sister organization, in another location, in another location?

- **Blue** – Ocean Strategy – Find out spaces where no competition is present, and proactively create opportunities. It can be for example, Opportunities that do not directly come under the purview of the Chief Information Officer such as legal process outsourcing, HR transformations etc.
- **Create Complete 'White Space Analysis'** – Depict the account map in terms of business units / horizontal units / strategic units – divisions / sub-divisions then identify the white spaces where you can focus your strengths for quick wins.
- Always create complete SWOT – Strengths, Weaknesses, Opportunities and Threats Analysis – Play at your strengths, identify your weak areas and work on corrective actions immediately, chase opportunities, and be aware of threats so that you can have the right strategy to prepare yourselves for the threats.

Strategic account planning is all about developing new ideas about how to grow the account in terms of customer satisfaction, loyalty, revenue, and margin. The purpose is to create a blueprint that helps the account team successfully implement the shared account strategy so everyone wins.

7. "Have Fun" – Organize fun activities / get-togethers (eg. Go to bowling together) to build right teams and strengthen team bonding.

To win "Team Building" is the key – Be a coach. Organize team building activities, it can be very simple. Include families if possible. This brings energy to the team and enable the right direction to achieve organization's goals.

8. Encourage yourself and your team for little extra effort.

Always encourage yourself and teams to do little extra effort, for example one sales call a day will make you to have additional 200 calls/year, Meeting one additional customer / prospect day will enable to build 200 new contacts per year. Remember the difference between a winner and a loser is miniscule (eg. In Olympic sprints, the difference in time between a winner and loser is fraction of seconds, but there is a big difference in prize money & medals). Simple things always make a difference.

9. Be humble, simple but Aggressive.

Always be humble in behavior and aggressive in achievements. You can think big, put enormous effort but be humble in behavior, but aggressive in achieving results.

7. Bringing Customers to Offshore (India or other nations) centers every quarter

Computers would be pointless if not the software that ran on them. Regardless of whether the software is operating system or accounting software, software sales is a big industry. Gone are the days when software was simply downloaded from the Internet or bought from the local store. With the boost in the software industry, software sales professionals are increasingly becoming people responsible for existence and popularity of various software products. As one of the fastest growing industries in the world, the software industry is reshaping the way sales in conducted around the globe. With globalization at its peak, industries have made use of the accessibility of new markets for their products. Software industry is already making use of this by outsourcing a part of their industry to the offshore regions.

The key role of any sales professional is to find businesses that can make use of the product or services offered by the company. A sales profession survives on the concept of "show and tell", where a product or service is shown to the potential buyer and then given an in-depth description of the product along with a narrative on how it can transform or add competitive edge to the buyer. The sales person provides a detailed account of the product and its advantages to its potential buyer. This is a challenge in itself but for software sales person, this is a bit more challenging as there is no definitive product to show. It is a rather tedious and challenging exercise where the sales professional has to get the potential buyer to give them a significant amount of time to present the product and illustrate its benefits to them. With a lot of companies relocated to offshore sites in countries like India, sales professionals find it difficult to get businesses to buy their software services as the process of "show and tell" is not only elaborate but also time and money intensive. The goal of this chapter is to discuss the need to bring customers to India or other offshore locations and sales tricks that can increase sales during such meetings.

The first task of the sales professional working in the offshore region is to identify the key players in the industry that would be interested in investing and buying the software solution for their business. Once you have narrowed down a list of potential buyers, an offline sales pitch needs to be designed which is impactful and creates the right amount of intrigue in buyers and they make the trip to India or other offshore locations for further discussions and the "show and tell" phase. As the software sales professional, you will need to follow the standard protocols used to lure potential buyers but additional effort like regular follow-ups, interaction with company managers and providing updated information regarding the software and related value-added services among other sales tactics need to be employed.

It is absolutely important that they make the trip to the offshore region, as it would give the software provider a chance to showcase their capabilities on their home turf. Furthermore, the buyers will be in a "captive mode", meaning that the representatives from the potential consumer company will be stuck with you and rely entirely on your company for the duration of their trip. This will help not only to showcase them with your capabilities as a software solution company but also give you an opportunity to show how your work is aligned with the vision and mission of the company.

The buyer learns some very inherent things about your company and witnesses the work life within your company. The buyer will be exposed to the product and functionality as well as observe the work culture that your company boasts. In order to get involved in any kind of relationship, especially professional, it is absolutely essential for 'culture' and sense of 'ethics' to match. Upon their visit to your company for discussions and negotiations, the buyer will be able to observe and establish whether their 'culture' and 'ethics' are in line with those of your company. The cultural experience is essential to create a healthy and friendly customer-partner environment. Once this relation is initiated, the buyer feels comfortable doing business with you. They begin to trust you and the sale of software and value-added services becomes comparatively easy thereafter.

As the software sales professional you are responsible to make sure they have a positive cultural experience with your company leading to a working relationship. Inviting international companies to offshore centers is difficult and involves a lot of planning and scheduling. Thus, software sales professionals need to be proactive and seize every opportunity for the possibility of the 'show and tell' exercise. In addition to the basic skills and habits discussed in previous chapters, the sales professional must also demonstrate the willingness to go the extra mile for their company's sales outcomes. In order to do so, you must make the habit of approaching potential businesses around the world to test the software solutions provided by your company and offer a cultural experience with the 'show and tell' exercise in India and other offshore centers.

Make every visit an 'experience' for them rather than a routine ritual. Capture those experiences. Personalize mementoes and gifts (caution is understanding customers gift policy and limits before). Make it traditional and do not shy away in showcasing your culture. Be proud about it. Never downgrade yourself, your organization, and your country!!

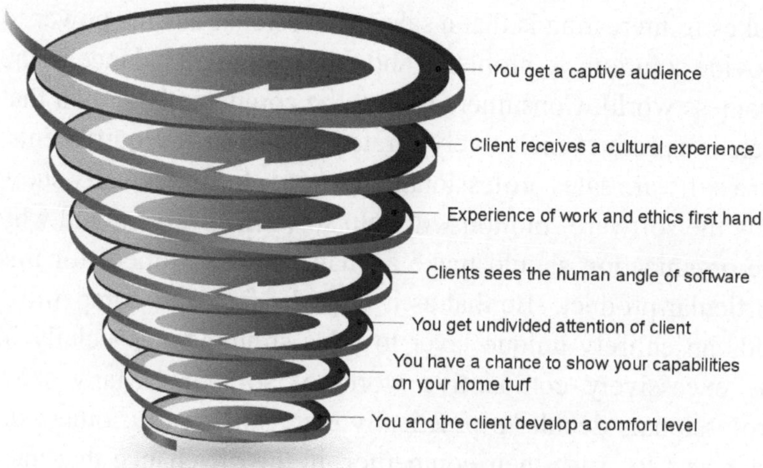

Fig: 8 – Benefits associated with inviting your clients to your offshore location

8. Handling competition

Sales has been considered an interesting profession. What makes it interesting is that a sales professional has the power to provide solutions to problems and thus creating a balance in the business world. Consumers need to be competently shown that there is a product exclusively curated to meet their requirements. As a software sales professional, one needs to strategically show how the software solution will help solve the problem and why the organization should make a financial commitment for this particular product. Be that as it may, the factor of competition adds an entirely unique layer to sales strategies, especially in the excessively competitive world of software. Many sales professionals decide to practically disregard rivalry; others do their best to crush their competitor, in the off chance that they come up amid the business cycle; yet others will even lie about it to prospects with an end goal to show it as being unreasonable. But, ancient Chinese military strategist Sun Tzu famously stated:

"Keep your friends close and your enemies closer."

Although it is true for every industry but in connection to the software sales deal it particularly stands true. Software industry is constantly evolving, and everyday various technology companies are developing an upgrade to the already existing software and revolutionize a whole section of the industry and displace well established players. Thus, as a software sales personnel it is absolutely critical to know everything conceivable about the competition in order to acquire business and to keep them from moving onto other companies. Equipped with that data, plan sales strategies to counter any measures the competition might take. Here are some tips to tackle software competitors:

Tips to Tackle software competitors	Know your Unique Value Proposition
	Prospect Perception
	Your relationships
	Customer Support
	Counter Tactics
	Find an Opportunity
	Conduct research about the company
	Underscore the low points
	Highlight the Solution you have to offer
	End the Habit

Fig: 9 – Tips to tackle software competitors

1. **Your Unique Value Proposition:** It is evident to most people that the basic fight to be won in a sales battle is to show the product as the absolute solution to the issue faced by the prospective buyer. The goal is to properly convey that the product you sell is unique and has characteristics that the rival's products lack. This is trickier when you're in a field with a few contenders who have a product with similar qualities. As a sales professional representing the company, you should endeavor to make a unique and lasting impression. One way is to offer additional advantages apart from the software, for example, a free trial of another advanced software technology that might be suitable for the company.
2. **Prospect Perception**: It is usually not enough to have an extraordinary offer, because there is a possibility that

your potential buyer isn't persuaded. It's insufficient for you to just make an offer, if you want to truly win your prospect organization over, it would be wise of you to counsel them and gain an insight into their real concerns and really comprehend how does your organization/item/benefit them. In this way, you would be able to work better and curate a sales pitch exclusively for them. While enquiring about their needs, you should also attempt to discover their opinion on your competitor. In this way you'll discover how your product or services truly stacks up in the focused area, for a specific requirement. Tactfully also inquire about the arrangements the opposition has displayed to the organization and why the organization is thinking about it or why they're most certainly not.

3. **Your Relationships:** In standing your ground against rivalry, connections mean the world. You could see sales connections as a kind of stepping stool, with "businessperson" at the base and "companion and accomplice" at the best. When you're nearer to the top, you'll discover immediately when the opposition has attempted to sneak into your prospect organization, for instance, and undermine your arrangement. With solid connection prospects your customers need to manage you, and will regularly make a special effort to keep away from your rivals. As you are cementing your connections, do all that you can to discover what sorts of connections have been worked at your prospect organization by your competitors? In the event that your opposition has been managing your prospect for quite a long time, you may need to prepare yourself for a tough climb. Be that as it may, at any rate you'll know. To win a client far from the competition, you might not want to pursue the higher authority immediately for a sales deal. Rather, you should

search for somebody persuasive inside the organization who could be your business champion. Since, they have access to the opposition's product and will be able to point the shortcomings of their product. They will be the most energetic for a change inside the association, and they are your intended interest groups. On the off chance that you can associate with them and transform them into a backer for your item, you're destined for success.

4. **Customer Support:** As your business cycle moves along, you ought to reliably be discovering how solid your position is with your prospect, versus that of your opposition. You should know this for each leader at your objective organization, and for any other person that could impact the purchasing choice.
5. **Counter Tactics:** On the off chance that you have examined your opposition well, you'll comprehend what kinds of strategies they're probably going to lock in. For instance underbidding may be a typical strategy. On the off chance that you have your connections entrenched with your prospect, you'll get some answers concerning an aggressive offer from them specifically before it goes exceptionally far and have the capacity to sound your prospect out: is your prospect organization liable to exploit a contender's arrangement? You would then be able to respond likewise. On the off chance that you know your opposition dependably uses such strategies you can even envision their technique and take them off before they even have the opportunity to strike. It is a smart thought to have countermeasures effectively settled for any moves your finishing may make.
6. **Find an Opportunity**: Once you've discovered your objective prospect, motivate them to trust in you about their present contract or involvement with the opposition. The initial step to prevailing upon prospects who are

existing clients of your rivals is discovering when their present contract is up. They're not going to break an agreement that terminates 8 months from now, so you have to approach the prospect at the right moment. You should get in touch with them a couple of months before the agreement is expiring, and plant the seed of progress. On the off chance that you miss this window and they renew the agreement, you're in a tight spot for a couple of more years – so ensure your planning is correct.

7. **Conduct research about the Company**: The more you know, the better prepared you will be to the point at which you converse with a leader, and push the deal to the next level. So you have to discover as much as you can at the present time from your champion, and some other sources you can get to. To what extent has this present prospect's organization been a client of the competitor? What item would they say they are utilizing? What are the typical difficulties caused by this item? What point would you be able to best hotshot your item from? This exploration will be unbelievably vital when you're prepared to pitch your item to somebody with specialist. In his book – "Competing Against Luck" – Harvard Business School professor Clayton Christenson talks about "Jobs Theory". He theorizes that customers "hire" products in order to perform a specific "job". He defines a "job" as "some progress that a customer is trying to make in a particular circumstance". As a sales professional, ask yourself: What "job" is my product going to do for this prospect? Why should they "hire" our product over competitor's?

8. **Underscore the low Points**: Since you have all the data you require, it's a great opportunity to contact the chief at the organization through your champion. This

is tied in with persuading the prospect that they require a change. In case you're endeavoring to supplant a settled in item, there's uplifting news – there are most likely numerous dangerous low points on which you can center. When conversing with a prospect that has a current arrangement, make a point to discuss issues that you know have come up finished the years. Since you comprehend your opposition so well and you've done your homework, you realize that the item is moderate, or doesn't offer the usefulness you do, or is altogether more costly. Make a point to underscore these prevalent issues focuses in your underlying call with the chief.

9. **Highlight the Solution you have to offer**: Since you have the chief's consideration and intrigue, it's a great opportunity to demo your answer – and you better be set up to influence your item to shine. On the off chance that you get this far with a contender's client, you're fit as a fiddle and can almost feel the new deal. Since, you are aware of the shortcomings of the current product and the client is keen on a change; use the knowledge to highlight how your software solution can tackle every need of the buyer. Demonstrate, through a demo, that you are aware of the problems they are facing and focus on how your item can be speedier, less demanding to utilize, or more affordable.
10. **End the Habit**: The hardest piece of winning a client from a contender is defeating the dread of the obscure. The reason such huge numbers of clients stay with their present, unacceptable sellers is on the grounds that they've put so much time and cash into it as of now. They know the item, and regardless of whether they don't care for it, they would prefer not to need to gain some new useful knowledge. You need to persuade them

that there are many, numerous advantages to changing to your item and it's justified regardless of the interest in preparing. In case you're ready to conquer that dread, you'll be praising your win quickly.

There's nothing sweeter than winning a client far from your greatest rivalry. These are not the most straightforward deals to close, but rather with the correct data, the "internal champion(s)", an incredible demo and the sky is the limit from there, you will be the victor at last. It's a definitive prize—you clash against your greatest rival in the business, and your organization prevails upon the client. Regardless of whether it's a small sale deal without much revenue net, the triumph is capable and fulfilling just due to the fact that you beat out the opposition. Be that as it may, this is simpler said than done. Regardless of whether you have a far reaching information of your greatest rival – furtively viewing their online classes, perusing their site, following their blog, and completing a broad focused examination – this doesn't ensure accomplishment with each prospect.

While tackling competition, software sales personnel make certain mistakes; here are the top three mistakes:

1. **Good product-market fit isn't enough**: Various managers in the industry have noted that in the present software market, it's imperative to characterize a client encounter that is 100 times superior to the present state of affairs. There are various explanations behind this, including the way that idleness, incumbency and management are for the most part conflicting with you. For developing organizations, this implies figuring out how to be exponentially better with less assets. Therefore, focus is vital. It has also been noted that organizations execute better when they aggressively organize and plan their endeavors. This often implies that hyper-focus

on the small company market where there is product-market fit. To succeed, fight the temptation to widen your concentration excessively or too early, and after that scale proportionately. What does this mean — "hyper-focusing … where we have the fit"? It implies seeking after those market sections for which your software or service offering has a one of a kind and convincing argument — exponentially superior to business as usual — and seeking after just those portions. Numerous private B2B organizations have created plans that are working for a subset of clients, however they are still tested with sales cycles longer than perfect. Normal income per client stays underneath the objective. Or on the other hand new client sales development is incremental, not exponential. Market fit can enhance from having all the more progressing discourse with clients. For focused areas, your answer may basically be only a decent to-have benefit and not sufficiently convincing to beat regular undertaking obstructions. With more market concentrate, organizations can locate a sweet spot by building up an intense comprehension of clients' needs in a specific portion, which is more nuanced than the more extensive part prerequisites.

2. **Are you competitively distraught?** : Competitors come in a wide range of shapes and sizes. As Zendesk CEO Mikkel Svane says, "There's a mind blowing assortment of programming items out there." Without a doubt, read the "About Us" area of the considerable number of organizations in your market universe, and consider what number of those view your space as theirs. Your rivals incorporate other privately owned businesses and bigger built up office-holders with monstrous sales associations. Competition also incorporates benefit and

exchanging organizations that speak to outsider sellers. It has been observed that 70% of on-premise software sales have customarily been channel-based. 80% of on-premise software merchants work a channel program to empower different organizations to offer their items, while just 20% of SaaS sellers work comparative projects. This channel and exchanging obstacle features an aggressive test for SaaS organizations going head to head against conventional programming companies. It's a zero-sum game among vendors, so marking a client implies a misfortune for another person. One frequently ignored advance is basically captivating with clients about the focused scene — including forthcoming and also win/loss targets. Spend time to gather important data about your rivals and adjust accordingly.

3. **Unfortunate timing:** With big business sales, timing can represent the deciding moment for an organization. Terrible planning in the B2B sales process can come from a few components. Here are three regular planning issues:
    - **Timing issue No. 1:** You're behind the market demand curve with a not-exponentially-better product — and losing to competitors. If you don't give clients adequate motivations to roll out an improvement, you will experience excessive complacency to close business. The client's default activity is to stay with their present deal. Be forceful in tackling this issue by revealing more interesting, earnest prerequisites, and after that soundly and proactively tending to those. More target focus and client driven product cycle can enable you to get ahead of the curve.
    - **Timing issue No. 2:** You're in front of the market demand curve and attempting to bring sales to a close. Venture

markets can be unwelcoming to pioneers, so consider discovering approaches to connect a dot in answer for your 'on top of things' plan. For instance, TigerText presented a protected endeavor versatile informing stage to human services clients in 2010 however confronted objection from doctor's facility representatives that still depended on pagers. To conquer this, they built up an informing arrangement that included paging choices. To get your foot in the door, you may need to help esteemed however conceivably obsolete prerequisites to enable organizations to progress to your stage.

- **Timing issue No. 3:** You're enduring under the heaviness of a long sales cycle and not settling enough negotiations rapidly enough.

Software and services sales is a challenging domain within sales. Since there are many companies developing same or similar software solutions, it is essentially the job of the sales professional to stand out in the competitive circle and sell it to potential businesses. There are numerous ways to stand out in the crowd but one of the basic steps to close a deal is to get businesses to recognize a problem and then showing them that problem is worth resolving. As if this is not hard enough, salespeople also have a third obstacle to overcome. They must help prospects understand why they are the best choice for the prospect's business. In a competitive market, standing out is a daunting task but through skills and finesse these hurdles can be overcome.

9. Contracts

A contract is a binding document, which outlines promises or a set of assurances that must be abided as an obligation, the failure of which may lead to legal action against the defiant member. Contracts made in sales are just like any contract signed in the business world and follow the same protocols. As a sales professional, one must demonstrate a deep understanding of contracts and key concerns associated with a sales contract. While making or signing any business contract i.e. sale summary, it is imperative to be aware of terms that are most imperious. This knowledge will enable a sales professional to stay away from issues with conflicting arguments or disputes and guarantee the benefits ensured in the sales contract.

A business contract is an agreement that lays out the terms and conditions of an exchange of software or service for payments. It recognizes:

- The purchaser;
- The seller;
- The software product or service offering; and
- Any other critical terms.

Notwithstanding these, there are a few more components that a sales professional should ceremonially focus on while making the business contracts.

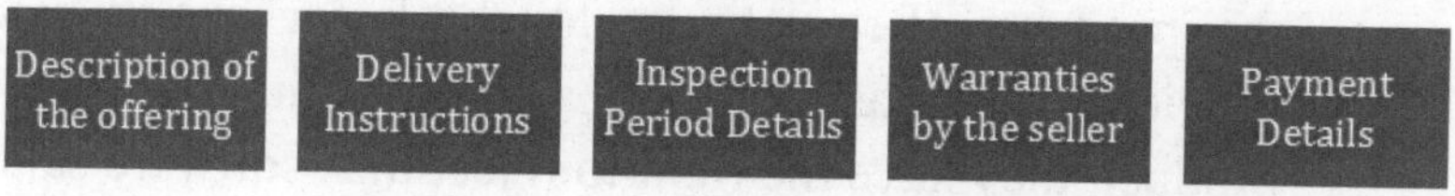

Fig: 10 – Key Components of all contracts

1. **Description of the Goods (Offering):** The depiction of the software or service offering is normally the most critical term in any business contract, which also stands true for sales contract. This is one aspect where there is possibility for oversight with regard to the depiction. As a productive sales professional, it is essential to make certain that it distinguishes the correct offering that the purchaser needs to buy and incorporates all the pertinent subtle elements, for example: type, licenses, modules etc. This will guarantee that the sales professional conveys the right offering with its ecosystem. Software sales professionals must describe their product in an effective manner, highlighting key attributes of a software.
2. **Delivery Instructions:** Another aspect that needs to be clear in order to have a successful sales contract is to provide clear delivery instructions. As a sales professional, one must ensure that the agreement is clear about the time and date of installation of software, which party is in charge of the risk of loss of the data or other current functionality during installation or use of the software etc. In case of sales, a lot of these concerns are minimized, however, the sales professional must clearly illustrate the delivery related concerns, which also includes the set-up, and installation related queries.
3. **Inspection Period:** Every product or offering undergoes an inspection period and many sales contracts forget to check the necessary time frame required for a particular period. This period gives the purchaser time to examine

the products after delivery to check for quality and efficiency. In case of any nonconforming software product, they have the right to reject it. A software sales professional must take into consideration factors that might not only positively affect but also negatively affect their sale contract during the inspection period.

4. **Warranties from the Seller:** Purchasers regularly disregard the assurances being made by the sales professional on behalf of the seller. Since there is a standardized method for warranty, the software sales professional must make clear statements with regard to warranty of software while making the sales pitch. The warranty related to the software's functionality, effectiveness, uniqueness must be clearly stated and in case of faulty software or discrepancy in the software or poor service quality in delivering the software, sales professional must provide a step-by-step recovery process in the contract. It should also give details about the individuals to be contacted in case of issues related to warranty.

5. **Payment Details:** It is an obvious element in a contract, which explicitly mentions details with regard to the payment of the product or services. However, software sales professionals must also bear in mind other payment related issues like installation charges. In addition to that, the contract must also answer any queries like: Will the software and services be paid for in portions or one single amount? Does the seller require a particular technique for installment? In the event that the purchaser won't pay immediately, it is necessary for them to provide a note to explain the payment terms. This will enable the sales professional to be transparent and show the company their work ethics and professionalism.

Contracts across domains are an integral part of businesses, and as sales professional with the target of selling software technologies to businesses, it becomes essential to understand and imbibe practices that will endorse the software product as well as the business. Software sales professionals must take extra care while curating the contract and ensure that all aspects are taken into consideration for expansive reach and growth of the software company across businesses.

Various types of contracts

Contracts come in a variety of ways – but as software sales professionals you should get very knowledgeable about two of them – Master Services Agreement (MSA) and Statement of Work (SOW).

Master Services Agreement

A Master Services Agreement is a contract that clearly documents key terms of engagement between the signing parties. Its purpose is to set a foundation to speed up and simplify future contracts. It specifies performance objectives and documents the responsibilities of both parties. It also lists the current and prospective services that will be covered by the agreement. MSAs typically state performance objectives as service level agreements -- written, measurable process or service performance targets that the software and service provider, and client agree on. MSAs help companies document and manage client expectations, clarify the roles and responsibilities of both parties, improve service delivery and build rapport.

MSAs present a good way to facilitate and simplify contract negotiations between the parties. With an MSA, a software or services provider and its customers work through most of the broad, but significant concerns that could make or break a contract upfront. Doing this negotiation ahead of time of a specific contract for a particular project or initiative, allows both parties to focus more on specific contractual concerns, such as price and time frame, when an actual contract arises. MSAs are often complex agreements full of legal language and require legal expertise from both parties. By negotiating MSA in advance, prior to any specific contract is under discussion, the parties avoid time pressures which will free up time to carefully identify and address any potential issues.

Typically an MSA takes weeks or months to negotiate and come to an agreement by both parties. It depends on the extent or scope of the agreement and the priority level it has with the involved parties. After a company deliberates through the MSA negotiation process once, it can more quickly identify and address those issues when negotiating the next MSA because it now understands the types of issues and concerns that arise.

Statement of Work

A Statement of Work (SOW) is a document within a contract such as Master Service Agreement that describes the work requirements for a specific project along with its performance expectations. SOW is primarily used to define the liabilities, responsibilities and work agreements between two parties, usually clients and service providers.

SOWs should be written in precise language that is relevant to the field of business. Software sales professionals should pay special attention in this aspect when writing SOW with their clients. This prevents misinterpretations of terms and requirements. In spite of being a detailed document, a SOW provides a general description of work and makes reference to supplementary documentation whenever further specifications of a particular task are needed.

A well-written SOW includes the scope and Key Performance Indicators (KPIs) for the agreement. Buyers will use these KPIs as a baseline to determine whether the service provider has met conditions of the SOW.

Thought references

- http://ecquire.com/blog/100-days-to-complete-sales-automation/
- **http://www.bakercommunications.com/sales-training/sales_professionals-Eleven-Habits-of-Highly-Successful-Sales-Professionals.htm**
- https://www.smei.org/?16
- http://www.top-travel-tips.com/business-trip-report.html
- http://www.brighthub.com/office/entrepreneurs/articles/105353.aspx
- https://blog.hubspot.com/sales/how-to-stand-out-from-the-competition
- http://work.chron.com/six-principles-selfmanagement-9912.html
- http://partnersforprogress.com/Articles/Self_ManagedTeams.pdf
- https://www.briantracy.com/blog/general/the-principles-of-self-management-part-one/
- https://websuccessteam.com/WSTblog/2014/10/manage-cycle-ups-downs-business/
- https://www.leadsquared.com/why-sales-tracking/
- https://www.legalnature.com/article-center/sales-contract/the-5-essential-elements-of-a-sales-contract
- http://www.lexisnexis.com/documents/

pdf/20150722022427_large.pdf

- http://blog.close.io/5-tips-for-selling-saas
- https://www.madetech.com/blog/why-a-single-source-of-truth-matters
- https://www.linkedin.com/pulse/20140528233246-2763081-single-source-of-truth-for-enterprise-it-systems/
- https://www.icertis.com/blog/enterprise-needs-single-source-truth/
- https://www.datapine.com/data-connectors/sugarcrm
- http://www.cignex.com/blog/integrating-sugarcrm-magento-e-commerce-platform-manage-customer-relationship
- http://blog.ring.io/why-sales-tracking-matters-and-how-to-do-it-right
- https://salesvue.com/the-importance-of-sales-reports/
- https://www.briantracy.com/blog/general/the-principles-of-self-management-part-one/
- https://www.salesforce.com/blog/2014/02/self-correcting-sales-person-gp.html
- http://partnersforprogress.com/Articles/Self_ManagedTeams.pdf
- http://work.chron.com/six-principles-selfmanagement-9912.html
- http://usir.salford.ac.uk/17280/1/20040000.pdf

Snapshot of Soft Skills!

- Identify your stake-holders and maintain positive relationships with them.
- First impressions are very important.
- Being on time is imperative. This means sticking to the schedule, each time. If you are late, let it be known well in advance.
- Take notes in meetings. You will be surprised what you forget.
- Know your boundaries. Talk with your supervisor about what decisions you should or should not make. Analyze/review expectations frequently
- Observe and learn others, yet create your own style. Be careful to not imbibe those traits that are likely to be detrimental.
- Have fun. Make friends. Enjoy what you do.
- Learn from your seniors on how they keep a track of the numerous tasks that they have to accomplish. Having a daily "To do" list helps.
- Before leaving messages on voice mail, write down your message and speak it slowly. For e-mails, learn when to do a "reply all" vs. "reply".
- Make a visible impact in first 100 days of your new role or job

- Understand that it is OK to do mistakes. Ensure that you don't repeat these mistakes.
- Anything that can be measured statistically can be improved. Find a way to implement measurability.
- Criticize in private and praise in public.
- Follow-up and follow-up some more. It will highlight your dedication like nothing else.
- A hand-written thank you note is far better than an e-mail.
- Differentiate yourself from your competition to provide value to your customers. And remember that both competitors and customers can be internal.
- Plan on Monday morning; then assess and take stock on Friday. Track your weekly status without fail.
- Recommend solutions to problems and challenges and identify opportunities.
- Focus on three sides of the triangle – Employees, Customers, and Understanding your company's Business.
- Awareness on priorities will change on daily/monthly basis. Plan proactively.

Raghu's Top Ten

1) Recognize that change is an inevitable aspect of life. Learn to accept changes.
2) Make friends, especially from other cultures. Take the best from cultures and understand others' worldviews. Embracing diversity is the key to being a people's manager.
3) Get to know your managers and introduce yourself.
4) Read as much as you can; and not just your textbooks – newspapers, journals, magazines, and books that pertain to your areas of interest.
5) Travel – this is the best way to know people from your country as well as those from other countries.
6) Make good use of time. Never let a chance go to enhance your education.
7) Set annual goals for to improve yourself. Have a Mission Statement as well as a Vision for your life.
8) Network extensively. Develop and maintain positive relationships with your family, coworkers, and managers in your work environment.
9) Get involved in some volunteer activities. Give back to your community and remember where you came from. Be in touch with your Alma Mater. Be socially responsible.
10) Leave your footprints on all aspects of your life (Employment, Education, and Family)

Client Account Planning for Sales Template

Section I – Executive Dashboard

Client Overview & Initiatives	• *Provide an overview of the Client business and any specific advantages enjoyed in the industry.* • *List projects or initiatives Client is executing to improve revenue, reduce cost, spur innovation, transform or reinvent to stay ahead of the competition*
Current Goals for this Client	• *Be specific about what you your immediate goals for this Client – value addition, innovation, cost reduction, transformation with investment*
Current Relationship with Client Business	• *Provide highlights of current relationship – supporting business critical processes, investment for mutual growth, adding value through improvements and innovation, software and service delivery excellence*
Account Risks & Mitigation	• *Identify the risks to your business with this Client and what actions by whom by when you should take to mitigate or eliminate the risks*
C-Level Relationship	• *Describe the relationship with C-Suite, Other Key Decision Makers and Influencers. You may want to use Color Code Red/Green/Yellow* • *See picture below*

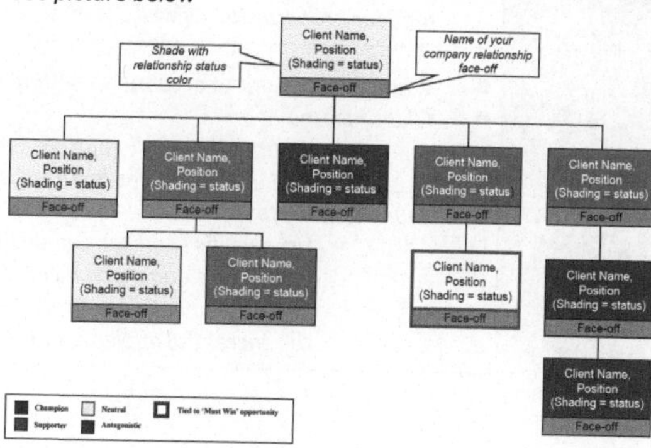

Client Advocacy	• *List the Net Promotor Score (NPS) you achieved at this Client and top 3 actions to improve it*
Opportunities	• *Identify Opportunities in specific software or service lines that are a good fit for the client along with when (quarter/year) they are likely to be awarded* • *Estimate Total Contract Value (one time, multi-year deal) of Opportunities*

Section II – Account Growth Strategy

Client Organ-ization Mapping	• *Get hold of the Client Organization Chart and map out the status of you/your company relationship starting at the top. You may want to use color coding to describe the status for easy visibility. Here are some examples of status you can use.* ○ *Champion, Tied to "Must Win" Opportunity, Supporter, Neutral, Antagonistic*
Current En-gagements	• *List all current engagements and status* • *Include Description, Revenue for the current year, Resource Cost for the year, Feedback Status (Green/Red/Yellow/Blue- Customer is delighted)*
Value Delivered to the Client	• *Summarize the business value that the account team has delivered to the Client as a result of successful projects*
Client Needs and Shared Account Growth Strategy	• *List the benefits that Client expects from a long term (3-5 years) perspective* • *What can we proactively offer to the Client to increase our strategic partnership?* • *Account growth strategy should be shared by both Client and you. It begins with the Client's goals and ends with how you can help them to achieve those goals. All the while ensure that the strategy is valuable for your organization as well.*
Account Strategy Objectives	• *What do you want to accomplish with this Client – in two dimensions* • *Client focused* ○ *What objectives/initiatives can help the Client achieve its business objectives and/or that map to its pressures* • *Your company focused* ○ *List specific short term and long term objectives - business growth, dislodging an incumbent, becoming a trusted partner, investments into Client's strategic priorities, repeating the successful implementation in another unit and so on*

<table>
<tr><td>Solution Map</td><td>

- *List Client business objectives and match your solutions better than competitors*

</td></tr>
<tr><td>Value Map</td><td>

- *Identify and Pursue Opportunities that provide High Value for both client and your company*
- *Create a two-dimensional grid – see the picture below*

<table>
<tr><th>#</th><th>Description</th><th>High Value Pursuit (Y/N)</th></tr>
<tr><td>1</td><td>Opportunity 1</td><td>Y</td></tr>
<tr><td>2</td><td>Opportunity 2</td><td>Y</td></tr>
<tr><td>3</td><td>Opportunity 3</td><td>N</td></tr>
<tr><td>4</td><td>Opportunity 4</td><td>Y</td></tr>
<tr><td>5</td><td>Opportunity 5</td><td>N</td></tr>
<tr><td>6</td><td>Opportunity 6</td><td>Y</td></tr>
<tr><td>7</td><td>Opportunity 7</td><td>Y</td></tr>
</table>

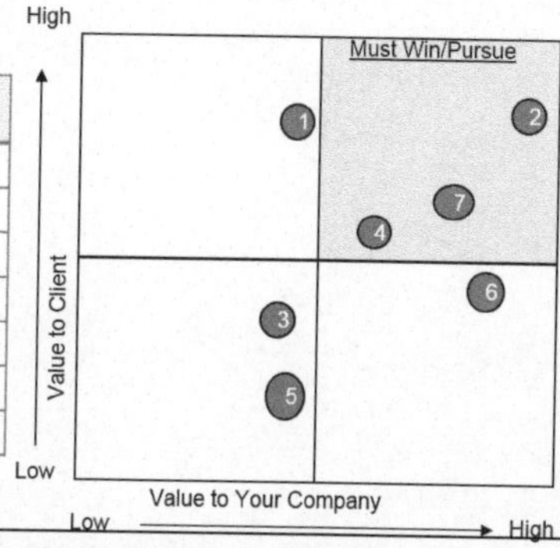

</td></tr>
<tr><td>Key Asks</td><td>

- *Provide a list of support actions (budget, resources, planning sessions, client referrals) you require from management to achieve account growth objectives*

</td></tr>
</table>

Other Books by Dr. Raghu Korrapati

What is civilization if not a vast and interlinked network of human relationships? With 'The Business of Good People', Dr. Raghu sets out to teach the reader how to make these relationships healthy and mutually beneficial. Dr. Raghu discusses certain characteristics that we all understand but fail to recognise their importance like punctuality, humility, politeness, rationality, prudence, self-supervision, persistence, apologising, assertiveness, taking the initiative, and sense of humour among others.

ISBN-10: 9350832577 **ISBN-13: 978-9350832578**

Leading an organization and its people to success remains a challenge for most managers. With organizations evolving and changing constantly it becomes even more difficult. Management theories and principles often do not provide solutions to the dilemmas that a manager has to deal with in the workplace.

This book by Dr. Raghu very adeptly gives some solid answers that managers have sought to be more successful at what they do.

ISBN-10: 8128837575 **ISBN-13: 978-8128837579**

This research applied Bayesian Modeling to medication noncompliance in glaucoma patients. A model-based decision support system using a Bayesian Network was developed to determine whether a patient was complying with the medications prescribed by the physician. The model may be generalized to other business situations where a decision has to be made based on incomplete and uncertain data sets. The purpose of this research was to devise a Bayesian framework to assess the compliance with medication in glaucoma patients.

ISBN-13: 978-0595368396 **ISBN-10: 0595368395**

This book is the essence of Dr Korrapati's 30 years of business management experience with highly successful multinational companies, coupled with distilled knowledge of his close interactions with great industry leaders. The book covers - developing a solid outsourcing strategy, deciding what to outsource, negotiating a good deal, keeping the engagement on track, ensuring access to the vendors' best resources, or even terminating a deal in a way that does not harm you. It will benefit everyone, whether you are from a firm that is looking to outsource or a vendor who seeks to establish his company as first choice partner for clients, to gain the advantage you are looking for in the fiercely competitive marketplace.

ASIN: B01JFV7JQM

Validated management Practices will walk you through the 108 required knowledge and skill areas sot that you can develop to balance the 3 critical aspects of management- employees, customers and financials, well. While some of the chapters in this book are oriented towards managers working in an Information Technology industry, it will be useful for managers in any industry with practical advice and tips on how to become an effective manager. In addition, the appendices contain extract of mandatory skills for all professionals from Dr Raghu's previous books - '108 pearls of Wisdom' and 'Dr Raghu's Top Ten' - his guiding principles.

ISBN-10: 9351654834 **ISBN-13: 978-9351654834**

While Dr Raghu Korrapati's 'Passage through India - A tryst with my soul' is an amalgam of Indian experiences of this widely travelled management guru, it is simultaneously also an exposition of his philosophical and spiritual ideas. So, as readers learn numerous lessons in sound management practice presented through Dr Raghu the leader's anecdotes and observations, he/she will be delighted to connect with Dr Raghu the man. Those familiar with Dr Raghu's previous works will be enthralled with another masterpiece on the art and science of management, this time in the context of the master's sojourn as the leader of an India IT organization. 'Passage through India' will, however, will also appeal to those who wish to understand the composer behind the composition, i.e, the mind of a man who successfully runs a large corporate organization.

ISBN-10: 9350836823 **ISBN-13: 978-9350836828**

Dr Raghu Korrapati's newest book is a seminal work that is bound to be soon accepted as a significant and powerful contribution to the literature on higher education. This is his landmark effort to encapsulate in one place all that a research scholar might need during his/her research, be it on any subject or discipline. The result is a complex and nuanced picture of the nature, processes, and contexts of research scholarship in varied departmental, disciplinary and institutional cultures.

Undoubtedly, this pivotal and pioneering book will prove to be valuable to both faculty and graduate students who study higher education. Further, institutional leaders, deans, and chairpersons of tenure, and promotion committees who seek to develop vaster comprehension of scholarship will also greatly benefit from this.

Dr Korrapati has mentored thousands of research students in a wide spectrum of disciplines and fields over the span of several decades. This book by him is the latest in a long line of works that have inspired and informed innumerable students and professionals across countries.

ISBN-10: 9352617614 **ISBN-13: 9789352617616**

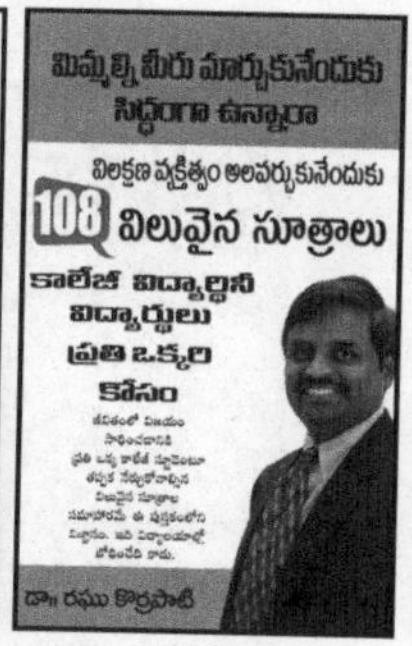

There is often a considerable gap between the aspirations that many college graduates harbor and the way they go about achieving their goals. While education and technical expertise are often ignore and that defines the difference between an average and a successful career. Dr. Raghu Korrapati has taken it upon himself to identify this 'soft' element and painstakingly elaborated upon its numerous facets. The result is this path-breaking book, which highlights the soft skills that every young graduate and professional needs to possess to reach the pinnacle of professional success. The 108 pearls of wisdom presented here have been drawn from sources as eclectic and diverse as Greek, Indian, Buddhist philosophies, modern day management theory, and psychology. This book has been translated into many languages.

ISBN-10: 8128834223 **ISBN-13: 978-8128834226**

Listed in Best Seller Category

A Master Service Agreement (MSA) is a contractual document that specifies performance objectives and outlines the responsibilities of both parties in the agreement. It also lists the current and prospective services to which the agreement applies. MSAs typically state performance objectives as service level agreements – written, measurable processes or service performance targets that the service provider and customer agree on. A statement of work (SOW) is a formal document that captures and defines the work activities, deliverables, and timeline a vendor must execute in performance of specified work for a client. The present study attempted to ascertain the factors in developing MSAs and SOWs and various best practices for alternate dispute resolutions available for offshore software managers. The study adds to the body of knowledge in the areas of Software Intellectual Property Rights, Alignment of MSAs and SOWs, ADR Mechanism for Contractual Breaches, Best Practices in Information Technology, Offshore Management, and Organizational Behavior.

ISBN-10: 1532020686 ISBN-13: 978-1532020681

The admission of foreign students to universities and colleges in the United States has two major components: the evaluation of foreign educational credentials, and the administrative process that converts the admission application into an enrolled student. The first component has historically been a source of much ambiguity and trouble for Indian students and professionals vying for places in USA Universities.

Dr Raghu Korrapati, in another glorious attempt at championing the cause of students and young professionals all over India, has come up with this seminal work to eliminate this ambiguity. In this ground-breaking book, he displays rare acumen, insight, and scholarly prowess to analyse the education systems in the USA and India, before going on to provide painstakingly researched information on each Indian higher education degree and its equivalency with respect to USA degrees. For this reason alone, this book is worth its weight in gold for any Indian student planning to study in the USA or an Indian professional aiming to work in the USA.

Apart from the students, there are numerous other institutions and individuals who will benefit from the wonderful content present in the book – USA admission officers and universities, USA employers hiring Indians on H1B visas, licensors, USA state/federal agencies, and immigration attorneys. The amount of detail on the USA education system that has been offered by the matchless Dr Korrapati will also help Indian educational administrators.

ISBN-10: 9352619870 **ISBN-13: 978-93-5261-987-0**

H-1B visas play a very important role in hiring foreign born skilled workers for Specialty Occupations in the United States. This visa system has largely benefited the U.S economy, benefitting the I.T industry the most, with the flow of skilled foreign-born employees. Due to the growing concerns over misuse and a perceived threat to domestic jobs, stricter scrutiny on H-1B petitions has increased in the past few years.

This book aims at demystifying the myths surrounding "Specialty Occupations" not only to the employers, but also to petitioners, academics, attorneys, students and other interested parties. It also aims at filling the gap in the research and understanding on Specialty Occupations. There is no comprehensive text or authority on this important issue and all the information available is only through the policy memoranda of USCIS, judgments in appealed petitioners and blogs of attorneys.

This book tries to provide a better understanding of the issue and also identifies some common errors in H-1B petitions and aims to be a one-stop reference to employers, attorneys and expert opinion evaluators on the issue

ISBN-10: 9352787708 ISBN-13: 978-93-5278-770-8

This book is updated version of previous years book. Based on receiving huge compliments from prior version, this book includes updates for years 2019-20. Several new guidelines in the area of Minimum Requirements for proffered position, Interview requirements for Specialty occupations questionnaire, sample job description templates, Guidelines on generic "Engineering" or "Business Administration" degrees, and new requirements for evaluators.

This book aims at demystifying the myths surrounding "Specialty Occupations" not only to the employers, but also to petitioners, academics, attorneys, students and other interested parties. It also aims at filling the gap in the research and understanding on Specialty Occupations. There is no comprehensive text or authority on this important issue and all the information available is only through the policy memoranda of USCIS, judgments in appealed petitioners and blogs of attorneys.

This book tries to provide a better understanding of the issue and also identifies some common errors in H-1B petitions and aims to be a one-stop reference to employers, attorneys and expert opinion evaluators on the issue.

ISBN-10: 9352969227 ISBN-13: 978-93-5296-922-7

There is tremendous ambiguity surrounding this field. It is compounded by the fact that grading systems differ widely in theory and practice from one country to another, and the fair interpretation of foreign grades into national ones is a major concern, both for students returning after a study period abroad and for university staff required to assess the credentials of foreign applicants. The academic world, especially students, struggle to determine what their education amounts to in another country.

The credential evaluation component also exists outside of the academic community: at state licensing boards and other types of governmental agencies, at professional associations, and at private foreign educational credential evaluation services which assist institutions and agencies that do not have in-house expertise. This book is also aimed to facilitate the smoother functioning of these institutions.

ISBN-10: 9352969219 ISBN-13: 978-93-5296-921-0

It is often said that salespeople would rather sell than spend a day learning how to do it. They think time is money and every hour spent in training is money lost and time wasted. But what they fail to understand is that learning how to do sales effectively is actually a catalyst for great sales results for the organization and excellent sales performance for the individual. It is worth noting that while sales is one of the easiest careers to get into, it is not as easy to sustain and spend a life in. So to put it in simpler words, ***"Everyone can be a sales person, but not everyone can be a successful sales person".*** To be a successful salesperson it is important to have a deep understanding of the industry you cater to. While the general skill set remains the same, it is the deeper and niche understanding that has the power to differentiate the best from the rest.

In the market, there are numerous books and articles on various sales techniques available. In this book, I am discussing the 'Nine habits of highly effective software sales professionals'. The title gives you a broad idea of what this book is all about, but more than nine habits, it is packed with 30 years of my personal and professional experience in the software industry and managing clients. I provided more emphasis on how successful sales professionals, sales leaders and their companies organize themselves with short-term and long-term planning and adopt disciplined execution on those plans.

ISBN-10: 9352969200 ISBN-13: 978-93-5296-920-3

Notes